Carola Milanis

The History of Catholicity in Stephenson County, Illinois

Carola Milanis

The History of Catholicity in Stephenson County, Illinois

ISBN/EAN: 9783744790772

Printed in Europe, USA, Canada, Australia, Japan

Cover: Foto ©ninafisch / pixelio.de

More available books at **www.hansebooks.com**

MOST REVEREND P. A. FEEHAN,
ARCHBISHOP OF CHICAGO.

THE

Golden Jubilee Souvenir.

THE HISTORY

OF

CATHOLICITY

IN STEPHENSON COUNTY,

ILLINOIS.

FREEPORT:
F. CHAS. DONOHUE, BOOK AND COMMERCIAL JOB PRINTER.
1896.

TO THOSE

BRAVE HEROES AND HEROINES OF FAITH AND PATRIOTISM,

THE CATHOLIC PIONEERS

OF STEPHENSON COUNTY,

THIS SIMPLE RECORD OF THEIR FIDELITY AND

ITS NOBLE RESULTS

IS AFFECTIONATELY DEDICATED.

Freeport, Illinois,
Feast of the Immaculate Conception, 1896.

PREFACE.

WHEN introduced to a stranger, who is henceforth to be an acquaintance, and perhaps a friend, one's impulse is to study the individual's countenance, to learn from each feature a trait of his character, and to judge from the expression gleaming in the eyes and lingering about the mouth, what sort of a moral and intellectual existence he has based upon that character.

A preface should not only introduce the book to us, but it should aid in that scrutiny of features and of expression which will make the book more than a mere acquaintance, so that we shall begin and continue its perusal in that spirit of friendliness which kindly overlooks imperfection, and, with affectionate pride, slightly magnifies excellence.

What, then, are the features of this little volume, between the covers of which you are about to glance, kind reader? Plain and homely it may be, but clear-cut, and bearing the impress of that honesty of purpose without which no face is truly attractive, no work truly noble. The expression that lights up these features and gives them a beauty, not intrinsically theirs, comes from the spirit of faith, and hope, and charity.

This book is to dwell in each home in St. Mary's parish; it is to be one of the household, a friend who cheers, by recalling sweet and sacred memories of the past, basing on them the still sweeter and more sacred hopes of the future.

If it enters homes in other parishes, it will be as a messenger bearing good tidings of exceeding great joy, and its voice will proclaim the worthy deeds of a noble people, urging those who welcome its message "to go and do likewise."

Thus it is sent forth, as a loving friend to one, as a kind messenger to another; may the welcome accorded it, by one and all, be as heartfelt and sincere as are the sentiments and motives that have given it an existence among the creations of the great literary world.

CAROLA MILANIS.

FACTORS
In the Life of the Catholic Church.

In the wonderful life of the Church of God, we find three grand factors: the militant, the suffering, and the triumphant armies of immortal souls. Of widely different characters, yet of almost equal powers, these magnificent factors, through the beautiful alliance of spiritual forces called the Communion of Saints, have effected glorious results which to-day illumine the world, radiating, as they do, from great beacon fires set blazing, (in many a critical epoch of the world's history) by saintly hands on towering mountain heights, and fanned, in our day, to a glowing heat and brightness by the profound thought and sacred eloquence of His Holiness, Leo XIII.

Revelation, that ineffably precious gift of an Infinite Intelligence to finite minds, has granted us much knowledge of that supreme factor in the Church's sacred activities, the triumphant souls in heaven, also of the powerful band of holy sufferers undergoing their purification. Faith assures us and we proclaim in the words of the Creed, our belief that the triumphant and the suffering souls fail not to fulfill, in behalf of the militant, many an office of grave import, while a union of the activities of the three mighty divisions of the Church furthers the grand work of religion. Though we shall ever bear in mind the silent workings and hidden influences of the other two, it is with the efforts, the struggles, and the labors of the militant factor that we are now concerned; these we are to study and to describe, these we hope to glorify.

More efforts are made, by the ordinary men and women

about us, with a direct intention to please God and to increase His ultimate glory, than we permit ourselves to believe. The Church Militant rests on its arms less frequently than we think; it is on guard more frequently than we realize. Much of the noble strife is silent; many of its shouts of victory are so clear and high that only the angels hear them.

Fascinating indeed is the study of the world's mighty conflicts; delightful is it to trace the great events of history to their sources, to unveil their causes, to discover their tendencies, to develop their results and to guage the full importance of their effects. Such studies are replete with interest and profit at any time, but the fascination, the delight, the interest and the profit are a hundred-fold increased when the events dwelt upon concern religion, when the influences under consideration effect changes in the moral world, when the causes lie mysteriously hidden in the Infinite Mind, when the results affect the destiny of immortal beings and all the tendencies are heavenward. Well indeed may the interest of such studies be thus increased tenfold and the profit thus become immeasurable.

The history of a locality comparatively insignificent, among earth's widespread nations and princely cities, might, if purely secular, be deemed somewhat unimportant, its value doubtful and its necessity a disputed point; but once introduce the factors mentioned above, but once let the Church and her mighty hosts of triumphant, suffering and militant souls enter into the consideration, then no locality is insignificant, no event of its history is unimportant. The value of such history, as giving glory to God and edification to souls, will be undisputed, hence our pages, devoted to the progress of Catholicity in Stephenson County, will bear information of superlative interest to the mind filled with the light of faith, and of immense value to the heart that is full of hope and charity. To the mind of God, and in the science of the saints, the souls existing in Stephenson County are of as great value as those enjoying life and its activities in New York, London, or Paris.

The loss of a soul in mountain solitude, or the triumph of

a soul in desert wilderness, the offering of Holy Mass in darkest Africa, or the giving of the sacraments to the savages of the Pacific islands, are events that far surpass in importance the victories of an Alexander or the triumphs of a Buonaparte.

Thus it is that matters which relate to the vast interests of immortal souls are not limited in importance, or lessened in value, by mere distances or boundary lines. Where souls are concerned, Heaven touches very closely upon earth; it is a transforming touch, too, causing temporal affairs to expand into eternal results, and the finite to gain everlasting possession of the Infinite. These noble, fundamental principles must be borne in mind by him who reads our simple account of more than fifty years in the life of the Church among simple, God-fearing people, in a locality unknown, perhaps, beyond the boundaries of our own State.

ST. MARY'S CHURCH, FREEPORT, ILL., 1896.
REV. W. A. HORAN, PASTOR.

Introduction of Catholicity into Illinois.

Can we doubt that the Church Triumphant, seeing all things in the Beatific Vision, watched, in ecstatic joy, the progress of the frail canoe that carried adown the great "Father of Waters" the weight of a nation's spiritual inheritance? We may well believe that never did king or queen, however great and powerful, make so royal and magnificent a progress through mighty kingdoms and rich cities, as that of the precursor of Christ in the Valley of the Mississippi, as that of the heaven-appointed bearer of glad tidings, as that of Father Marquette through primeval forests, over virgin prairies, and on the waters of unknown rivers. Since all worldly pomp and ceremony were lacking, the more were heavenly visitants attracted. The greater the simplicity, from a human point of view, the greater the invisible glory of the joyous guard of angelic beings established about the sainted missionary and, the more lonely his pathway, the more magnificent were the winged processions of glad spirits that followed him, as in the name of God most high, he took possession of the virgin soil of Illinois. Here, amid bands of scattered savages, he planted the tiny seed that, among civilized growths, has become so stately a tree. Of its fruitful development we have evidence in the prosperity of the Archdiocese of Chicago and its dependent dioceses of Alton, Belleville and Peoria, for not only to the savage children of the forests did Father Marquette bring his heavenly message; sacred tradition, that never failing voice of the Holy Spirit, bore it down through the centuries to the white settlers. They had brought with them their faith, it was strengthened by words and hymns still re-echoing through the sweet, untainted air which the saintly one had set in vibration.

And now—where once were Indian farms, are flourishing dioceses; where wigwams stood, tower the steeples of stately cathedrals.

We read, in books of varied titles and by different authors, the same sweet story of Father Marquette's journey down the Mississippi; of his return, in 1673, with his companion, Joliet, a Canadian merchant, and of their brief stay with the tribe of the Peorias.

His promise to this tribe that he would return to establish a mission among them and "the gentle Illini" was kept, late in the year 1674. With that admirable courage that always distinguished him, the devoted priest started from the Straits of Mackinaw, crossed Lake Michigan and then passed along its western shore until, worn out in body, but indefatigable in soul, he reached the mouth of the "Chicagou." Not being able to proceed on his way to the expectant tribes of the Illinois valley, he sent a messenger to inform them of the fact, and many of them hastened to his side, happy to be of service to him, until such time as his restoration to health should enable him to become of infinitely greater service to them. His holy ministrations brought spiritual joy, and the peace of God, to the inhabitants of many an Indian village, before he again turned his face towards the north and began his last journey through the wilderness. Illinois was, at that time, a wide, uncultivated territory, teeming with rich promises of the agricultural wealth of the future. It had then no white inhabitants, but they were not to be long in coming nor were they slow, when once arrived, in rendering this one of the fairest and richest of the great states; neither did they fail to devote part of its noble resources to the support and to the propagation of the faith.

Illinois is now dotted, over all its extent, with church edifices, and, everywhere that the number of children requires it and means render it possible, a school stands beside the church, as outworks beside a citadel, for mutual support and protection.

Early History of Catholicity in Chicago.

Like the gleam of the fire-fly in the twilight, was the brief delay of Father Marquette at the mouth of the "Chicagou;" the light of faith and fervor did not again illumine the spot, until one hundred and fifty years had elapsed. The locality became known, successively, as a traders' point, a government reservation, and a frontier outpost. Here Fort Dearborn was built, for the protection of the few white settlers against their red enemies. In times of peace, to this point came the Indians to claim the supplies of goods and of money promised them by the government in exchange for their lands. Here too came the Jesuit missionaries, also Father Baden and others, from Bardstown, Ky., and Vincennes, Ind., the religious priests seeking to convert the Indians, and the secular clergy endeavoring to give temporary spiritual comfort to the Catholic soldiers and traders stationed at this outpost.

The missionary period of the seventeenth century passed away; but not until 1833 did the church in Chicago become permanently established. Its present life and strength originated in the efforts of Father St. Cyr, authorized by Bishop Rosati of St. Louis, to take charge of the two hundred souls constituting the Catholic population of the town growing up at that time on the spot where Father Marquette had paused to preach and to pray in 1674. It required two weeks of unpleasant traveling for Father St. Cyr to reach the mission at Chicago, nor did he find much at his journey's end to rest or comfort him. From Bishop Rosati he had recived a letter of appointment, commanding him to "report to the Bishop of Chicago, when Chicago should have a Bishop"! None but a prophetic soul could have seen, at that time, in the wild little town, any of the characteristics of a bishopric.

The first episcopal visit to Chicago was that of Bishop Brute of Vincennes, Ind., who gave confirmation to the few persons who had presented themselves to Father St. Cyr for preparation. The congregation comprised, at that period, the paschal season of 1835, four hundred souls of various nationalities, French, Irish, German, American and Canadian, all of whom attended the services in the poor little frame edifice called "St. Mary's of the Lake"; to these services there likewise came, quite frequently, the Commandant, accompanied by his staff and by the garrison of the fort. This was the embryo, as it were, of the towering and wide-spreading tree, to whose rich growth we have already referred. Later in the same year, 1835, came the famous rush of Irish emigrants, from seaport towns, to the village beside the great lake. This was caused by the proposed construction of a canal to join the waters of Lake Michigan with those of the Illinois river. The numbers who came so greatly increased Father St. Cyr's flock that he was obliged to appeal to the bishop for help in ministering to so great a number of souls. Assistance was granted him and to his own were joined the labors of Rev. Fathers de St. Palais, Fischer, Schaefer and Dupontavice. The last named took charge of Joliet, and two Vincentian Fathers of the Mission devoted themselves to the faithful residing at LaSalle. The other Rev. Fathers named above, together with Father St. Cyr, found plenty to do along the course of the canal, the construction of which brought the Catholic laborers to a different point almost daily, making of them a sort of wandering or pilgrim congregation gathering in camps, in cabins and in log huts to assist at a service no whit different, in essentials from, that which is to-day celebrated, with so much pomp and glory, in the handsome cathedral of the Holy Name. Sore need had the poor people of the sacred comfort that only religion could afford them, for those were the dread days of the cholera, which were followed by the financial disasters of 1837.

In 1844, when its population had become 12,000 and a number of small towns had sprung up in its vicinity. Chicago was raised to the dignity of an episcopal see, with Rt. Rev. William Quarter as bishop. The varied events of his administration are the subjects of very interesting chapters in "The Souvenir Volume of the Silver Jubilee of Archbishop Feehan." St. Mary's Church, in Chicago, which was to have been Bishop Quarter's cathedral, was in an unfinished condition, at the time of his arrival, and even lacked the requisite furniture for sanctuary and altar; moreover, there was a considerable debt on it, for the payment of which there seemed absolutely no provision. However, the Bishop and his brother, Very Rev. Walter Quarter, having united their personal funds, to pay off the three or four thousand dollars due on the work already accomplished, the people were encouraged to contribute sufficient amounts to complete the structure. Not long after the bishop's arrival, then, the cathedral was finished, and it was his happy privilege to send towering to the sky, its cross-laden steeple, the first to point heavenward from a church in Chicago. It is needless to dwell upon the rapid and marvellous changes in the diocese, since that time. The advancement and improvement that edifies and delights us, at this hour, began in Bishop Quarter's administration, and though he continued only four years his sacred duty to the young flock scattered throughout Illinois, yet the ordination of twenty-nine priests, and the erection of thirty churches, constituted but a small part of his arduous labors during that brief, but exceedingly fruitful period. "He began with six clergymen in his diocese, and not even one ecclesiastical student; he left after him forty priests, besides twenty students preparing for the priesthood, while on the many improvements which he had originated there was not a cent of debt." Poverty and privation had been the portion of priests and people, this had been cheerfully shared by their bishop, and he united with them in transforming hardships, by patient endurance, into the unfailing riches and abundance of eternal dwelling places.

Our space will not permit us to enter into details regarding the administrations of Bishop Quarter's successors, but we hope our readers will not fail to become acquainted with the contents of the volume we have already recommended, where they will find the labors of Rt. Rev. Jas. Van de Velde, Rt. Rev. A. O. Regan, Rt. Rev. Jas. Duggan, Rt. Rev. Thos. Foley, and Mt. Rev. P. A. Feehan, eloquently portrayed.

The diocese of Chicago now enjoys the spiritual services of three hundred and fifty-five priests; its churches number two hundred and twenty-eight; of chapels there are one hundred and six; one hundred and forty institutions afford educational advantages to Catholic youth, and seventeen are devoted to charity.

Forty-three thousand pupils attend the Catholic schools, academies and colleges and the population of the diocese numbers four hundred and eighty thousand souls. Among them many nationalities are represented, Irish, German and Bohemian predominating.

A quotation from one of the many eloquent addresses presented to His Grace of Chicago, on the occasion of his Silver Jubilee will correctly indicate the origin of the present prosperity of his important charge, "These churches, schools and charitable institutions stand as monuments to the earnestness and generosity of the Catholic population. They are built by the voluntary contributions of the people, by the personal sacrifices and savings of zealous priests, by the untiring industry, self-denial and economy of devoted brothers and nuns. They evidence the influence which the Catholic faith exercises, where people are in possession of civil and religious liberty. They testify what can be accomplished, by a believing flock, when unhampered by state influence or interference—what can be done by a free church in a free state."

Perhaps in no diocese has the truth of the above been more evident than in that of Chicago. The church, in our county, is an off-shoot of that great tree of which our parish of St. Mary's is a sturdy, healthy, fruitful branch, and now we will do a little reverent botanizing—tracing from soil to root, from root to tree, from tree to branch, the sacred life of religion in Stephenson County, Illinois.

THE EARLY HISTORY

Of Catholicity in Stephenson County.

The nature of the soil, if only it be watered by the dews of divine grace, or by the crimson floods of martyrdom, matters little to the growth of the Church. So watered, and with men of truly apostolic spirit to till it, richly productive has been the soil of every part of our great country, from ocean to ocean, and from gulf to great lakes.

Each locality, in that wide expanse, has its beautiful history of suffering and self-sacrifice, joyfully offered in behalf of religious prosperity; our own region is no exception; many a beautiful incident might be recorded in proof of the devotedness of the Catholics of Stephenson County in early days. The angels of God keep the record of these deeds, though earth may bear no memorial of them.

A monument marks the spot where occurred the Black Hawk War, but no stately shaft or noble pile of stones marks the place, in the immediate neighborhood of this memorial, where occurred an event infinitely greater than any war, however serious in its results. All devout souls will agree in regarding the celebration of the sacred mysteries as immeasurably greater in importance and value than any event in profane history. Yet the solid memorial of the dread Indian war has no companion monument to tell the passer-by that here was offered, for the first time in our county, the Holy Sacrifice of the Mass. The sacred ceremony took place in the house of one Simon Brady, near Kellogg's Grove, and Father Stephen Vincent Baden was the celebrant. This was in October, 1827, as the good priest was on his way to visit Galena and Prairie du Chien, in which places miners were even then seeking for lead.

Six or eight years later, the Bishop of St. Louis, under whose jurisdiction the western part of Illinois had been placed, sent Father John McMahan to locate his dwelling in Galena and to attend the spiritual needs of the Catholics scattered throughout this section of the State. After a brief visit to Dubuque, Iowa, Father McMahan devoted himself to the service of the eight hundred Catholics in and about Galena. Authorities differ as to the date, but it was either in 1833 or 1834. The devoted priest's pastorate was short indeed, for he had labored only nine months among his flock, when God took him to his everlasting rest. His successor, Father Fitz Morris, was even a shorter time among the sorrowing people; in three months he followed his predecessor to the realms of eternity. His successor was Father Shanahan, who likewise departed this life while attending the spiritual needs of the early settlers of Galena. The bodies of these three priests, the first to die in our part of the country, were buried in the public cemetery, where they still lie, though it was proposed, in 1843, to remove them to the Catholic cemetery, that year opened for the burial of bodies consecrated by the sacraments of the Church.

Previous to the coming of Father McMahan, in 1832 or '34, Galena and Dubuque had been visited by Rev. Samuel Mazzuchelli, an Italian Dominician missionary, so well known and so beloved, in Wisconsin, Iowa and Illinois, that his life and labors constitute a sacred tradition rendering it unnecessary to repeat the events of the one or to describe the extent of the others in this work. Suffice it to state, in this relation, that one of the many church edifices built by him was St. Michael's in Galena, in which our brief history has an interest, because, from 1827 to 1843, the Catholics of Stephenson County were dependent upon the priests located at Galena for occasional opportunities to assist at the Holy Sacrifice and to receive the sacraments.

It was in 1835, after the death of Fathers McMahan, Fitz Morris and Shanahan, that Father Mazzuchelli laid the corner

THE NEW CHURCH AT IRISH GROVE.　　THE OLD CHURCH AT LENA.
　THE OLD CHURCH AT IRISH GROVE.　　THE CHURCH AT NEW DUBLIN.

stone of St. Michael's church in Galena; he then went to Wisconsin and his place in Galena was successively filled by Fathers Petiot, Brady, Oslangenberg and McCorick. It is well remembered by old settlers, that, in 1841, Father Petiot said Mass in the house of Michael Walsh, for the Catholic people of Irish Grove. The house is now owned by James Spellmann. From 1841 to 1846 Irish Grove was attended by the priest residing at New Dublin, and the services were held in private houses. Then a church was built which continued in use until 1895, when Rev. Michael Sullivan, the present pastor, replaced it by the fine frame structure of which the present congregation are so justly proud.

MARY HOGAN, OF NEW DUBLIN.

Our special interest in the Galena congregation ceases with the year 1843, in which Stephenson County received the services of its first resident priest, Father Derwin, appointed by the Bishop of St. Louis to the parish of New Dublin. The welcome pastor made his home with a family named Murphy and offered the Holy Mass in a log church, "16 ft. x 24 ft. and seven logs high," which had been erected in 1836. In 1844, the Bishop of Chicago was given jurisdiction over all Illinois, and, in 1846, he appointed Rev. Jas. Cavanaugh to the charge of New Dublin and the missions in its vicinity. This clergyman was succeeded by Rev. F. Kalvalege, who erected, in 1855, the church now in use in New Dublin.

THE EARLY
Catholic Settlers in Stephenson County.

Heroism has many phases and is variously developed by courage and by fortitude. The heroism of the battlefield is easily recognized and rarely fails to meet with the reward of fame; the brave soldier, the sturdy sailor, the gallant fireman—these are heroes whose right to applause is never questioned, and among them any manly man would gladly be classed, but there is a silent heroism, a hidden fortitude, an unproclaimed courage in many spheres of human action that escape the ordinary observer and are seldom recorded on the pages of history. Such was the heroism of the explorer, such the fortitude of a pioneer's wife, such the courage of the pioneer himself. Ah, those early settlers! those brave men and women who severed the ties of kindred and of friendship, who uprooted the fondest affections for place and people to go into strange lands and among savage tribes in search of a home, in search of a support denied them elsewhere. If we pause to reflect upon the condition of things, in the early part of our century, we will not hesitate to recognize the heroism it required to settle on the prairies of Illinois, or in the forests of Wisconsin, and to make one's way, sometimes with nature, and more times against her, towards the foundation of a home. A thousand difficulties, unknown in our day, and therefore not to be realized by us, rose up in the pathway of the first settlers striving to gain mere subsistence, where prosperity now offers freely the richest gifts. We would be ungrateful indeed, were we to forget those whose sacrifices and labors secured for us an inheritance of faith and prosperity. All honor then to the early settlers of our county and our town! We fain would see their names, not only recorded in this little book but inscribed upon monuments of marble in letters of gold! Think of the absence of physical comforts, of the dearth of mental food, of the loneliness and even desolation. Above all and before all, with the Catholic pioneer, ranked spiritual comforts and food for the soul, yet how frequently these were lacking, so that we find him, with his family, walking long miles over rough country roads, to assist at Holy Mass,

THE LATE GEN. GEO. W. JONES, OF DUBUQUE.

or selling his last cow in order to donate his share towards the erection of a log church, near his own farm and amid the simple homes of his neighbors, each of whom had made similar sacrifices to gain benefits ranked by him above all other blessings.

In 1832, when the late lamented General Jones, of Dubuque, visited the Black Hawk battle-fields, in search of the remains of Col. Dufresne, his brother-in-law, he met with Father E. Brady, a pioneer priest of Michigan, and they together visited what remained of the house in which was celebrated the first Mass offered in Stephenson County.

This, as we have elsewhere stated, was the home of Simon Brady, the first Catholic settler in our county, he having located here in 1827. He was a cousin of Father Brady, mentioned above, and is remembered as a devout and faithful son of the Church, esteeming himself more highly honored by the offering of the Holy Sacrifice under his roof than if he had entertained all the kings of Europe.

THE LATE MR. AND MRS. THOMAS BARRON.

Some of our citizens may remember Freeport's first court house, also the fact that its foundation was laid by James Burns and William Kilpatrick, who came here in 1836. The former bought from the U. S. government forty acres of land, bordering on the river, on a portion of which the Brewster House now stands; the latter purchased a hundred and sixty acres upon which the greater part of Freeport is built. James Burns, having sold his property, went to Ireland, about 1841, and was there married to Miss Kate Barry, in 1845. Returning to Freeport in

1850, he made here his home and proved himself a worthy member of St. Mary's parish.

William Kirkpatrick remained in Freeport until 1844 or '45, after which he resided in Canada, where he went in company with the Cavanaugh Brothers of Dublin.

Edmund Mullarkey and family came from Indiana in 1836, and settled in Irish Grove. Daniel and Anthony, sons of Edmund Mullarkey, are still prominent members of that parish and identify themselves with every religious and charitable undertaking. Mrs. Sartori, nee Kate Mullarkey, a descendent of Edmund's, is a resident of LeMars, Iowa, where she takes an active part in religious, charitable and educational affairs. She was this year elected president of the Ladies' Auxiliary Committee of the Western Summer School at Madison, Wis. She was educated at St. Clara's Academy, Sinsinawa, Wis. Portraits of Messrs. Anthony and Daniel Mullarkey and of their wives will be found in this work.

In the same year, 1836, the following old settlers and their families came to Stephenson County, viz: Thomas, Patrick and Michael Flynn, Robert and George Cavanaugh, John Glynn, James, Nicholas, Michael and Peter Fenlon.

Rev. Father Petiot said Mass in Michael Walsh's log house in 1841; this was the first time the Holy Sacrifice was offered in Irish Grove; the house now belongs to James Spellmann.

In 1842 there came to the county, with their families, Michael Stenson, Martin Mullin, Thomas Brie, Thomas Cuff, Thomas Fox, Thomas Flemming, Thomas Howley, Patrick Richardson, John Blaney, Patrick Bradley, Matthew Reedy, Michael Blimm, Peter Mullin, Austin O'Malley, Thomas Slack, Martin and James Fitzpatrick, James Owens, Denis O'Donavan, Denis and Edward Doonan, Patrick O'Malley, Matthew Doyle, John Ginnenwein, John Spellmann, William Marlow and Maurice Hyland.

The last named settled in Rock Run township in 1846, where he now possesses a fine farm which he purchased, in those old days, directly from the government. Many a time his log dwelling was not only the abiding place of the priest of God but the

PATRICK FINN.   MICHAEL NOLAN.   MICHAEL MOONEY.
               JAMES O'BRIEN.
MICHAEL KENNEDY. ANDREW FAY.   MICHAEL STACK.

shelter under which was offered the Holy Sacrifice of the Mass.

During the time that elapsed between the years 1842 and 1850, homes were built in Stephenson County, for themselves and families, by the following faithful members of God's Church:

MRS. CATHERINE EGAN.
Sister of the lamented Rev. John Cavanaugh, the pioneer Priest.

John and Michael Graham, Denis Hawkins, M. Muligan, John Carty, John Maloney, J. Daley, Edward Crowe, Thomas McDonough, M. Geary, Martin Sughrove, Edward Kealy, James Murry, James Cullen, Charles Hopkins, Edward McNally, W. Rowen,.

William Gray, John Tracey, James Sullivan, Michael O'Leary, James Cox, John Herrington, Thomas Cashman, Thomas Keenan, Thomas McGuire, William McGurk, John Barron, Philip Hogan, Michael O'Boyle, Moses McGrath, Patrick Callen, Mary O'Sullivan, Patrick Moulton, Richard Gould, Elizabeth Cavanaugh, Lawrence Murphy, John Scanlan, John Kennedy, Robert Moran, Robert Franey, Catherine Murphy, George Murphy, Thomas Summers, John McNamara, Dennis Cavanaugh, Wm. Dunn, Bart Doyle, Francis Higgins, Christopher Hughes, Mary Murphy, John Menlove, Stephen Byrne, John Mullarkey, Dennis Quinlan, Edward Higgins, J. B. Vale, A. Malloy, H. Collins, W. Kinney, W. T. Cox, James Murphy, Pat Parron, Pat O'Brien, James Campbell, Frances Foley, Robert Wall, A. Hawley, Thomas Hawkins, Patrick Hawkins, Daniel Hawley, John Walsh, Joseph Carey, Charles O'Neil, Joseph Hays, James Hays, Jacob Burns, John Murray, James McCauley, C. Cummings, J. Cooney, Wm. Hamilton, Miles O'Brien, Ellen Doran, David Graham, John Graham, John Daley, Thomas Flemming, Peter Began, Jane Kelly, Thomas Howley, Annie Kern, A. McKenny, Thomas Kelly, Patrick Giblin, Dan Cavanaugh, John Howe, Patrick Lucy, James Kugan, James O'Brien, John O'Brien, Mat Carmody, James Cavanaugh, William Gould, Dan Brown, Andrew Farrell, Dennis Meagher, Michael Donovan, John Flanagan, Michael Reed, Thomas Reed, Michael Bowler, Pat Burns, Martin Byrnes, John Eagan, John McLaughlin, Bernard McCarthy, John Howes, Michael Laughlin, John Gannon, John Buckly, Patrick McGrane, James Barry, Joseph Pere, Windel Miller, Michael Mitchell, Matthias Kishermer, Matt Hettinger, John Hettinger, George Lamm, Philip Hamm, Andrew Hamm, William Hamm, Mr. Nohe, Henry Pifer, Joe Miller, Henry Lichtenberger, George Lichtenberger, Michael Bangasser, George Bangasser, Adam Rippberger, Peter Altes, Anthony Schaedel, Dony Schaedel, Joe Rapple, George Bruehler, Thomas Barron, William Barron, James O'Brien, John Foley, Patrick Hanafin, Bernard Coyle, Walter Barry, James Cavanaugh, Mrs. Carroll, Mr. Vail, John Loftus, John Martin, James Sullivan.

1850 TO 1860.—Wm. Osborne, Patrick Lacey, J. J. Sweeney, Dennis Sweeney, James McCarthy, John O'Brien, Dennis O'Connell, John O'Connor, Michael Cowley, Michael Ryan, John Lane, Patrick Carrigan, Michael Kennedy, Patrick Silk, Thomas Glavin, Bernard McGuire, John Collins, James Hart, John Crossen, Peter Bordaux, Patrick Kelly, John Keenan, Anthony Gavin, Morris Wingert, Bernard Devy, Patrick Hannifan, John Fanon, Patrick Riley, William Power, Thomas O'Connor, John Rapp, John Hensing, Robert Moran, Peter O'Regan, Dennis Murphy, Patrick Henry, Edward Connelly, Brien Casey, John Mahony, Carroll Fitzgibbons, Michael Nohe, John McGinnis, Richard Drever, George Shady, Michael Madegan, Dennis Haskens, Joseph Bar, John Lammon, Martin Lally, Patrick Mayly, Patrick Naton, Wm. Mannin, Thomas Fitzpatrick, Thomas Hollis, Martin Crowe, Wm. Lawler, Andrew Williams, Thomas Cashman, Edward Lynch, Robert Welsh, James Cox, Laurence Lyons, James Lenard, Thomas Keily, Michael Flar, John Power, John Sullivan, Thomas Hasset, Richard Hughes, John Sheehan, John Mahan, Martin Sordan, Michael Cowley, Thomas Ryan, James Kane, Michael Maher, James Casey, James Boyle, John Regan, Martin Fitzpatrick, Patrick McGrane, Patrick Mackin, Peter Grady, William Sheehan, George Scott, Matthew O'Neal, John Vail, Patrick McGrath, Pat McGuinnis, Thomas Gordon, Michael Broderick, Thomas Mooney, Joseph Rapple, Philip Steffen, James Hanahan, Thomas Grant, Patrick Silk, Richard Goff, Wm. Hyde, Richard McCale, Pat Dougherty, Thomas Gray, Martin McAndrews, James Darrah, George Blust, John Lyons, James Nolin, Thomas Lane, James Hogan, Bernard Casey, Richard Madigan, Anton Rodemeyer, Patrick McCoy, John Loftus, James Welch, Daniel Allen, Moses Burns, James Kane, John McDonnell, Robert Welch, Thomas Craton, Patrick Garreton, Thomas O'Connell, Joseph Brewster, Pat Hanafin, Pat Casey, Wm. Gallagher, M. Mullin, Cornelius Murphy, John McCalligot, Bernard Deery, James Keogh, James Cavanaugh, Patrick Root, Martin Lawless, Tom Barry, John McGinity, Pat Farrell, James Flanagan, John Wall, James McCarthy, Andrew Williams, John Reddington,

THE LATE MRS. MARGARET WALL.

Patrick Cawley, Patrick Hamilton, John Lahey, James Lahey, Joseph Lambert, James Hanagan, Timothy Coffee, Michael Dady, James Simson, Nicholas Glynn, Wm. Connell, Patrick Laly, Dennis Sweeney, Patrick Brennan, John Carr, Stephen Rigney, Christopher Skelley, Richard Dunn, Edward Mullaney, Pat McGovern, Dan Brown, Lawrence Seifert, M. Schneider, Pat Keenan, James Grace, Wm. Lahey, Thomas Brady, James Daley, Owen McCarthy, Pat Ward, Dan Kane, John McNerney, Edward Joyce.

These are a part of the great number of families that settled in this county before 1860.

The Foundation of St. Mary's Parish,

FREEPORT, ILL.

"An old meadow can be ploughed in straight furrows, but in 'a clearing' the plough must be turned aside for stumps and be lifted over rocks." There is much homely wisdom in this assertion of an author whose name we cannot now recall, and it contains a figure suggestive of the work done in pioneer days for religion as well as for agriculture. The devoted priests who dwelt in our county, from 1836 to 1855, worked in "the clearing"; they felled the trees, as it were, and prepared not only the harvest fields, but the pathways which were to become, ere long, highways to a then undreamed of prosperity. The soil has proved good, but in the "30's" and "40's," and the "50's," only a divinely enlightened eye, or prophetic spirit, could have discerned its value, for during that time the "clearing" was full of the stumps of human difficulty and of rocks of providential placing, such as God uses to test the strength of His chosen servants, but there were never wanting skillful, willing hands, under the guidance of wise heads, to turn the plough around the stumps or to lift it o'er the rocks.

The pastors of St. Mary's Church, from the earliest date to the present time, were Rev. Ferdinand Kalvelage (July, 1854–July, 1859), Rev. Thomas O'Gara (August 1859–March, 1866,) Rev. Fathers Westkamp and Fischer (assistants to Father Kalvelage), Rev. Thomas Kennedy (March, 1866–September, 1866), Rev. George Rigby (September, 1866–March, 1867), Rev. M. J. Hanley (March, 1867–August, 1869), Rev. P. L. Hendricks (August, 1869–February, 1870), Rev. F. J. Murtah (February,

1870–May, 1871), Rev. M. Stack (May, 1871–April, 1877), Rev. Thomas Mangan (April, 1877–October, 1887), Rev. M. Welby (October, 1877–February, 1890), and Rev. W. A. Horan (February, 1890——).

REV. FERDINAND KALVALAGE,
The second Pastor of St. Mary's Church.

In 1854 Rev. Jas. Cavanaugh came to Freeport as its first resident pastor, and in 1855 the first Catholic church, "old St. Mary's," a plain frame building, was erected by the joint congregation of Germans and Irish. Father Kalvelage, as was mentioned above, took charge of the parish in 1859, and when the

MR. AND MRS. P. M'GRATH.
MR. AND MRS. WM. VAIL.
MR. AND MRS. HUGH CLARK.
MR. AND MRS. D. O'CONNELL.
MR. AND MRS. M. FAGAN.

parishes were divided, in 1862, he continued in charge of the German congregation, which had, in the meantime, completed another church and had it dedicated under the patronage of St. Joseph. Father O'Gara became pastor of St. Mary's after this separation.

For Rev. Father Hanley, the people erected a comfortable brick residence, which Father Stack, with unselfish zeal, gave to the Sisters for a dwelling place, while he took up his abode in the attic of the school building. In course of time he caused the original St. Mary's Convent to be constructed, also the first St. Mary's Parochial School. The Sisters, Dominicans from Sinsinawa, numbered four, a music teacher and two teachers for the school, also one to oversee household affairs. During Father Stack's pastorate there was a vigor in the life of the parish that had excellent results.

Father Mangan's ten years were distinguished by several excellent improvements; the cemetery was surveyed, plotted and beautified, the church was raised and otherwise repaired, and an addition was built to the pastoral residence.

Rev. Father Welby, who was highly revered by his people, died while absent from his parish, on a journey taken for the benefit of his health. Father Horan, who had taken charge of the parish during Father Welby's absence, succeeded him as pastor.

Such, in brief, is the history of the "old St. Mary's"; simple indeed, but nothing is great in itself; it is only the doing of it that makes it great, and to such greatness the simplest deeds lend themselves. God does not care for mere results; what He does care for is the nice workmanship which our human personality has the power to lavish on the indifferent materials of an ordinary life and from which the finest results may originate.

Our readers will find it interesting, we do not doubt, to review the biographical sketches that appeared in a local paper, at the time of the dedication of the present church, hence we repeat them here, in addition to the brief statements made on the previous pages, regarding the labors of St. Mary's pastors:

MRS. M. MAHAN.   MRS. O'ROURKE.
MRS. HANAFIN.   MRS. HAGERTY.   MRS. R. CASEY.
MRS. M. DELANEY.   MRS. GARVEY.   MRS. JOHANAH NOLAN.

RECORDS OF THE PASTORS.

In the modest home of James Cavanaugh and Mary Keogh, his wife, in county West Meath, Ireland, was born a son in the year 1823. He was christened John, and his early days were spent in rural simplicity, for his father was a farmer and toiled early and late for the sustenance of his little flock. It was in this atmosphere that the boy took on the lines of character which characterized him as a man. It was here, too, that he received an education in hardihood eminently fitting him to take up his life work in a new section of America.

When seven years old the lad began attending school near his home. Three years later, he started for Mellingar, Carlow college, at which institution he studied until thirteen years of age. Next he attended college at Rheims, France, for seven years, and then entered the All Hallows College, near Dublin, where he remained about three years. During his entire school life, he showed himself to be an earnest student and made rapid progress in pursuing the course of study prescribed in each institution that he attended.

In 1846 he set his face westward, landing at New York city and going directly from there to Chicago. At the latter place he was ordained a priest, by Bishop Quarter, in 1847.

Soon after his ordination Father Cavanaugh came west to this county and located at New Dublin. His mission included New Dublin, Freeport, Irish Grove and the Fenlon settlement, north of Davis. Of these places only two—New Dublin and Irish Grove—had church edifices. Besides the parishes named, he filled occasional appointments at Elizabeth, Rockford, Mt. Carroll, Plum River, Savanna, Warren, what is now called Durand, and to all parts of the present congressional district, where families or congregations of Catholics had settled. He had four distinct residences: with Mrs. Catharine Egan, his sister, at Freeport; Mrs. Murphy, New Dublin; Edward Mullarkey, Irish Grove, and Peter Fenlon, at the Fenlon settlement.

His time was fully occupied in going from mission to mission, administering, with unfailing energy and zeal, to the

MR. AND MRS. MOSES BURNS.
MR. AND MRS. JOHN VAIL. MR. AND MRS. CHAS. M'COY.
MR. AND MRS. WM. OSBNRNE. MR. AND MRS. PETER MULLEN.
MR. AND MRS. JOHN LANE.

spiritual needs of the scattered Catholic families. Numerous sick calls, requiring long journeys, by night as well as by day, were faithfully attended, his sacred powers, as a Catholic priest, making it his imperative duty to respond, at any hour, and under any circumstance, to the call of persons in danger of death.

He continued in the discharge of his laborious duties at Freeport, until the summer of 1854, where, as directed by his Bishop, he took charge of St. George's, the only church, at that time, in Joliet, Illinois.

He was a man of great natural talent and many acquired gifts. His sympathetic nature and his ardent zeal made him untiring in his efforts for the temporal and spiritual welfare of those committed to his care.

He was in Joliet but a year and a half, when he was appointed to Alton, from which place, after a short stay, he departed to take charge of a church in St. Joseph, Mo. After a brief pastorate there, he returned to this section of the country, to bid his old parishioners good-bye. In 1859, intending to set sail for France, he went to New Orleans, but having stopped there to attend the Yellow fever victims, he fell a martyr to charity, and was found dead at his post.

Soon after his death, Mrs. Egan, who still lives in Freeport, received from the pastor, and from the Archbishop of New Orleans, kind and sympathetic letters, in which Father Cavanaugh's great zeal and his devotion to duty, in the midst of the plague, as well as his edifying death, were vividly described. He was greatly attached to his sister and her husband, and while in Joliet sent them several volumes of "Lives of the Saints," in which is written on the fly leaf, in a bold, flowing hand, "A gift from the Rev. John Cavanaugh, P. P., of Joliet, to his brother-in-law, Thomas Egan, and Catharine, his sister."

Besides superintending the building of the first Catholic church in Freeport, and raising funds to meet the expense, he began a fine house of worship at Alton, Ill., which was finished by his successor.

PASTORS WHO HAVE SERVED IN THIS SECTION.

Rev. Fr. WALKER.

Rev. Fr. STACK.

Rev. Fr. MURTAUGH.

Rev. Fr. MANGAN.

Rev. Fr. WELBY.

Rev. Fr. RYAN.

Rev. Fr. KEARNEY.

Rev. Fr. SULLIVAN.

During Father Cavanaugh's pastorate in Freeport there were no railroads. Early in the fifties, the Illinois Central was not yet completed, and he had to travel almost constantly with horse and buggy. The cholera made his work yet more laborious, because of the great number of sick people he was called upon to see. He met with many ludicrous and sometimes very dangerous adventures, in his travels over the wild country. Everywhere he found open for him opportunities for earnest work, and it is no wonder that he was greatly beloved by the members of his flock, for he was untiring in his efforts in their behalf.

FATHER FERDINAND KALVALEGE was born at Lohne, Oldenburg, Germany, June 27, 1829. He is a son of Henry and Catharine Kalvalege, and is an uncle of Father Clement Kalvalege, of St. Joseph's Catholic church. He attended school at his home and after coming to this country, in 1847, pursued his studies at Girardeau, Mo. Later he took up the course at St. Mary's of the Lake, Chicago.

He was ordained June 11, 1854, and his first mission was at Freeport, which place he reached July 22, 1854. He remained in charge of St. Mary's congregation until July 18, 1859. It was during his administration that the brick church, a decided improvement upon the little frame structure, was built.

At the same time he secured a suitable building and established a school for the children of his parish, though, at that period, parochial schools were not obligatory.

On leaving Freeport, Father Kalvalege went to Chicago, where he erected St. Frances' church, also its commodious school building and comfortable parochial residence.

Of fine abilities, greatly improved by an excellent education, Father Kalvalege was ever an earnest and successful worker in behalf of any good cause that enlisted his sympathies. His death was widely lamented and his memory is held in high esteem.

FATHER THOMAS O'GARA was Father Kalvalege's successor. Coming to St. Mary's in August, 1859, he showed himself, during the seven years of his pastorate, to be an indefatigable worker and a most zealous pastor.

Not being acquainted with the German language, he engaged, from time to time, the services of a German priest, for the benefit of those members of the congregation who spoke or understood that language better than they did the English.

Rev. Father B. Herderer, Rev. J. Mehlman, Rev. J. Uhlana, Rev. P. Fischer, and Rev. J. Westkamp were among those who gave Father O'Gara assistance in this manner.

It was during his pastorate that the congregations separated, the Germans building St. Joseph's church, and the Irish retaining the use of St. Mary's, after having given a certain sum to aid in the building of St. Joseph's.

The frame church, which had been vacated in Father Kalvalege's time, was immediately and effectively converted into a parochial residence, through Father O'Gara's efforts. He likewise secured property for St. Mary's cemetery.

The period during which Father O'Gara was St. Mary's pastor was marked by trials and difficulties, yet he always met them squarely, and displayed an admirable zeal, promptness, and diligence in the discharge of his duties. Agreeable to meet, witty in conversation, and edifying under all circumstances, he was highly esteemed by his people, who felt for him a warm friendship, for "to know him was to love him," as somebody said recently, in referring to his remarkable qualities.

Not less remarkable was his success in raising funds; besides paying off the entire indebtedness of the parish, and keeping its buildings in a respectable state of repair, he collected a sum sufficient for the purchase of the pipe organ which has ever since afforded St. Mary's excellent choir with equally excellent accompaniments.

Father O'Gara was transferred, in 1866, to Bloomington, Ill., a much more important charge, and there he erected a magnificent church which a cyclone demolished, almost immediately after its completion.

FATHER THOMAS KENNEDY succeeded to the pastorate of St. Mary's church, coming here in April, 1866, and leaving again in November of that year. He did not like the position from the first. His brief pastorate does not permit the chronicling of any changes in school, church or parochial house.

FATHER GEORGE RIGBY was the next pastor of St. Mary's, coming here in November, 1866, and leaving in the early part of the year 1867. Neither written nor traditional historical reources furnish authentic data regarding the events of Father Rigby's pastorate, and there seems to have been no changes in church affairs during the few months that he was in Freeport.

FATHER MICHAEL J. HANLEY came to St. Mary's to take charge of the parish in 1867. Zealous and self-sacrificing, he spared no effort to effect a satisfactory arrangement of parish affairs. Possessed of great energy and an undaunted perseverance, he accomplished much good in a brief space of time.

The old frame parochial residence having become unfit for the purpose, it was moved out of the way, and, on a newly purchased lot, was erected a two-story brick which continued in use until vacated by Father Stack for the accommodation of the Sisters. Father Hanley also had fences erected and shade trees planted. On his departure from Freeport in 1869,

FATHER P. L. HENDERICK succeeded him. The new pastor remained but a short time, during which there were no changes, and left in February, 1870, to be succeeded by

REV. F. J. MURTAUGH, a pastor ever zealous and active in the discharge of his duties. He desired to have a parish school connected with the church, and no sacrifice was too great for him to make in accomplishing that object. A fine two-story brick school house, capable of accommodating two hundred pupils, stood on a lot almost in front of the parochial residence and had been advertised for sale. It was purchased and the lot near it was soon after bought for school purposes. It was also during his time that the interior of the church was painted. He was highly esteemed by his people, who appreciated his efforts in behalf of both church and school. In June, 1871, he was succeeded by

FATHER MURICE STACK. Father Stack first turned his attention to the school, which he set to work to improve and

MR. D. SWEENEY.		MR. P. LACY.	MR. JOHN CAMPBELL.
MRS. J. CAMPBELL.		MRS. P. GLEASON.	MRS. P. LAHEY.
MR. P. LAHEY.	MRS. LACEY.	MRS. D. SWEENEY.	MR. P. GLEASON.

bring up to a high standard. Money was raised with which the building was repaired and duly furnished. Application was then made to the Dominican mother house, at Sinsinawa Mound, for instructors, who were supplied and immediately took charge of the school. He vacated his own house that the sisters might have a home, and then began to build them the present convent, which at that time was considered one of the most comfortably furnished structures of the kind in the north-west. In March, 1877, Father Stack was transferred to St. Mary's church, Aurora, Illinois. It was during Father Stack's administration that the church and the community sustained a serious loss in the death of Charles McCoy, brother to ex-Alderman A. J. McCoy. His devotion to the interests of St. Mary's is kindly remembered by many of the old timers.

No pastor of St. Mary's parish was more highly regarded than Father Stack. During his career, in Freeport, he never ceased to labor to improve the condition of St. Mary's church and school, and he contributed one of the handsome windows that adorn the new edifice. He is now in charge of the church at Fulton, Illinois, where he is universally respected.

FATHER THOMAS F. MANGAN was the successor of Father Stack. The new pastor soon realized that both the church and school needed costly repairs and he went to work immediately to make them. The very foundations, no less than the roofs and intermediate parts, required immediate attention. The roof of the church needing shingles, advantage was taken of the opportunity to raise it to a higher and more imposing pitch. The cost was considerable, but was not regretted, when the dark wooden gables were replaced by well lighted brick ones, in keeping with the rest of the structure. When the great improvement in the appearance of the church was manifested, all felt that the money had been well invested. During Father Mangan's administration of affairs a piece of land, containing about two acres, was purchased and added to the cemetery, which is now in a very respectable condition. Father Mangan was a diligent worker, who labored industriously for the congregation and the school,

MRS. P. JORDAN,
MRS. P. GRANT,
MRS. V. HOGAN,
MRS. J. B. J. DU FOUR.

MRS. P. CAREY,
MRS. J. CAVANAUGH,
MRS. JOHANAH BURNS,
MRS. T. GRANT.

raising more money for necessary expenses and improvements than would have been required for a new building, had all the congregation agreed to erect one. Father Mangan was pastor ten years, or until 1887, when he was assigned to Joliet, where he is in charge of a large congregation, and is holding likewise the responsible position of dean of the diocese.

FATHER MICHAEL WELBY reached Freeport Oct. 28, 1889, from the cathedral in Chicago. He was a man of great learning, who had long been connected with the church in America, and was warmly welcomed by St. Mary's parish. It was during his time that the matter of building a new church was considered, and a fair was held to create a fund for the purpose.

Father Welby was not a man of robust strength, and early in January, 1890, he made a trip to the City of Mexico, with a view to improving his health. Father Horan came here from Chicago to take charge during the pastor's absence. Soon after his departure—on the 18th of the same month, indeed—Father Welby died. The sad information reached the people through Father Kalvalege, and their sorrowful surprise was indescribable. A meeting of the principal parishioners was immediately called and they requested Father Horan to represent them in showing proper respect to their deceased pastor, hence he, accompanied by Father Hayes of Chicago, was to have proceeded to the City of Mexico and to have brought with them, on their return, the revered body of the dead priest. Owing to opposition on the part of the civil authorities, the object of Father Horan and Father Hayes was defeated; they were not permitted to remove the remains from Mexico. Prior to his departure Father Welby had made a will, and when proofs of his death arrived, it was learned that Father C. Kalvalege was named as executor. Among the bequests was that of $1,000 for the use of St. Mary's church, which gave evidence of his appreciation of the good people of St. Mary's congregation and was a token that his heart was in his work. Father Welby had many friends outside the pale of his own church, and his people valued him highly for his many excellent traits of character, as well as for his zeal and kindness.

Father Welby was a native of Ireland, from which country he came to America when he was quite young. He was ordained in Santa Fe, N. M., about twenty-five years before his death, which occurred in his sixtieth year. He had traveled extensively and had officiated in many celebrated Catholic churches and cathedrals of America. During his last years, but before coming to Freeport, he spent much time in Aurora and at the Chicago cathedral.

The people could not gain possession of his remains, but they cherished their pastor's memory and celebrated his funeral services with all the pomp and solemnity possible.

In these brief sketches of the pastors of St. Mary's there is much to edify, much to remember with pious pleasure and affectionate respect.

PIONEER CATHOLICS OF STEPHENSON COUNTY.

History of St. Mary's New Church.

We have already outlined the origin of St. Mary's parish and referred to the churches which preceded the present handsome structure, but before beginning an account of the remarkable history of the new St. Mary's, it may be well to lightly scan the record of the

FIRST CATHOLIC CONGREGATION AND CHURCH IN THIS CITY.

Father Cavanaugh was the first priest to be permanently stationed in the county, and his territory was almost unbounded in extent. His main station, however, was at New Dublin, but in 1853 he was transferred to Freeport.

It was in the little parlor of the home of Thomas Egan, where Montague & Hoyman's store stands, and at a time when there were but few houses in the new town of Freeport, that a number of Catholics met one afternoon to form a congregation. It was in that same little parlor, thanks to the generosity of Mrs. Egan, that services were held by her good brother, Father Cavanaugh. The congregation soon outgrew the place and larger quarters had to be found. Among those at the meeting were: Father Cavanaugh, Richard and Thomas Barron, Robert Balow, Mr. Tuhey, Edward Cavanaugh, James Manion, George Cavanaugh, Thomas and John O'Connor, Thomas Egan, Mr. Nagle, William Barron and Mrs. Catharine Egan. They had assembled to take action in regard to building a church, and all put down their names, for contributions, in accordance with their means. Thus were a few hundred dollars raised, but the sum was inadequate to the building of a new church.

In the meantime, the brave little congregation was granted the use of a hall belonging to J. K. Brewster, now of Colorado, who is kindly remembered in this connection by all of St. Mary's parishioners. The hall proved large enough for the Catholic citizens to assemble there to assist at the Holy Sacrifice on Sundays, and there they worshiped, until the little frame church, begun nine months later, was completed.

Various materials were voluntarily furnished and thus the expense was considerably lessened. Robert and Thomas McGee furnished the sills, others gave shingles, glass, nails, putty, etc., and so, after much labor and self-denial, the little structure was completed, and who shall express the happiness of a devout people, such as these, when they knelt once more in a real church, however poor and plain?

THE SECOND CHURCH.

It was during the pastorate of Rev. Father F. Kalvalege that the second church, a brick structure, was built. The new edifice was a decided improvement on the old one and was considered a grand building at that time, yet its low roof and dark wooden gables greatly detracted from the interior appearance.

The corner-stone was laid in July, 1855, and in it was placed a tin box which contained copies of the weekly papers of the city, some manuscript, 3, 5 and 10 cent pieces and a copy of the New York Catholic Zeitung.

The lumber used in the building was brought down the Mississippi to Savanna and hauled from there by oxen. The material was hewn out with the ax. The structure was 40 x 80 feet, with basement, and was finished on the common sense style. From time to time improvements were made on the building, which stood thirty-five years, or until the present grand structure was begun.

BUILDING OF THE NEW CHURCH—HOW IT WAS ACCOMPLISHED.

The people of St. Mary's congregation long desired and expressed a wish that they might have a new church. The old

edifice, at the time it was built, thirty-five years before, was no doubt a very beautiful structure, but it had not only outstood its time but was not large enough to seat comfortably the growing congregation that gathered within its portals.

There had been considerable church talk, during the time of Father Welby's pastorate and before it, but nothing definite had been done. The task of building a church was considered very great and many members of the congregation argued that they were too poor to erect a suitable structure, hence they were in favor of waiting for a better opportunity and more abundant means. The one was nearer and more easily attainable than they supposed, for a master mind was at hand. Rev. William A. Horan, on coming to Freeport to take temporary charge of St. Mary's parish, was requested by the pastor, Father Welby, to ascertain the sentiment of the people regarding the erection of a new church. All they had done towards it, under Father Welby's direction, was to appoint a committee and to hold a fair to secure funds. On acceding to Fr. Welby's request, Fr. Horan met with nothing but apathy and indifference, on the part of the people. Nothing more was done for awhile. In the meantime, Father Welby died and Father Horan was assigned to the charge.

Father Horan came to Freeport that he might escape the poison-laden atmosphere of the great city, and enjoy health-giving air of the country. He had planned for himself a thorough course of reading, but the field presented greater work than he had anticipated, hence, with that unselfishness characteristic of him, all thoughts of reading, and all other plans that he had made, were brushed aside, that he might enter, heart and hand, into the work of building the new St. Mary's church. He met with success from the start. The mighty obstacles that seemed at first to threaten the project melted away, as snow before the sun, and the expectations of even the most imaginative were exceeded by what he accomplished. It is a wonderful work—the work of an enthusiastic church builder, and it has not been excelled, all circumstances considered, by the achievement of any other clergyman in the country.

MR. ED. NOLAN.   MRS. M NOLAN.   MR. BANGASSER.
MR. J. FENLON.   MRS. E SHERIDAN.   MRS. BANGASSER.
MR. J. PECK.   MR. G. ROTZLER.   MR. H. LICHTENBERGER.

When the members of the congregation discovered what they could do, if united, they grew enthusiastic. A meeting of the old church building committee was held. Father Horan explained to them what might be done on the monthly donation plan, and, in order to secure perfect unity among the members of the congregation, a mission was conducted by Dominican Fathers.

In January, 1890, it had been decided to publish, each month, statements of the money contributed, and in April, 1890, at the close of the mission, Father Horan announced, one Sunday morning, that if forty families gave $250 each, they could begin and finish the church that year. Those who would make this contribution should bear, he smilingly said, the highly honorable title, "The Forty Martyrs!" He further remarked that it was simple folly to begin the erection of a church, without several thousand dollars in the bank. That afternoon there was a meeting of the congregation held in the church. And what a meeting it was! Father Horan presented a check for $250, and called on the others to do likewise. That day tested the generosity of the Irish heart, for $10,000 in solid cash was raised, and Father Horan announced that he would immediately begin the erection of the required edifice.

The proceedings of that Sunday proved that St. Mary's congregation meant business.

THE WORK BEGUN.

The required amount having been raised, the contract was let, by the building committee, in May, 1890, to William Ascher, who began his work by pulling down the old parochial house and the old church. During the time of construction, the school house, with a temporary wing, was used for church purposes.

The following building committee was selected: Rev. Father Horan, president; John Tracy, treasurer; Thos. D. Osborne, secretary; Patrick Grant, Thomas Grant, Michael Scanlan, Robert Casey, Richard Sheridan, F. Chas. Donohue, Michael Cowley, Jeremiah Riordan, Michael O'Brien, Wm. R. Barron, Michael Root, George W. Farnum, J. B. J. DuFour, James Darrah, John

E. Hogan, R. R. Hughes, A. J. McCoy, Thomas J. Foley, John Sullivan, Chas. McNamara. A few months afterwards, much to the regret of all, Patrick Grant, of the committee, always one of the most earnest of workers, was called from this world to his eternal reward.

The work of razing the buildings progressed rapidly. The house was torn down, and the church was being demolished, when the whole city was shocked to hear that the walls had fallen and killed many of the workmen. Later it was found that none were killed, but that five had been more or less seriously injured. Father Horan himself had a narrow escape; he was standing, at the time, at the door of the church; while there, he noticed the absence of supports, and was about to call attention to the fact when the crash came. Had he entered the building, he could not have escaped being killed.

THE CONTRACTS.

The tearing down and clearing away was continued rapidly, and in June, Wm. Ascher, who had secured the stone work for $1,900, began the foundation. R. D. Dirksen had taken the carpenter work for $6,000, and began it in the latter part of July. The super-structure of stone was awarded to Wm. Ascher for $8,000, so he continued that work right along from the foundation, with Herman Hanke in charge. The other contracts were: M. Scanlan, plastering, $1,400; Janssen & Son, painting, $1,800; D. Dasso, Chicago decorating, $500; Bartlett Hardware Co., steam fitting, $1,860; J. J. Wade, Chicago, gas piping, $170; Williamson & Schroeder, gas fixtures, $380; Bartlett Hardware Co., plumbing, about $400; pews, $1,105; Waddell Bros., altars, $275; pulpit, $75; confessionals, $60; sanctuary furniture, $80; carpeting and matting, $360.

SOME MONEY MATTERS.

To the cost of the building, Father Horan contributed over $3,500. Every cent of church revenue he devoted to the one grand purpose, besides being a liberal contributor to it from his personal bank account. The following is a list of the principal donations, besides which there were many special offerings:

1890		1890	
January	$ 144 00	November	$1,390 80
February	276 00	December	927 00
March	437 00	Christmas offering	340 00
April	349 00	1891	
May	10,027 00	January	1,478 00
June	532 00	February	2,667 25
July	371 00	March	1,715 75
August	749 00	April	692 00
September	1,031 75	Easter offering	573 25
October	1,693 50	May	370 00

SOME SPECIAL DONATIONS.

The stained glass windows, presented by zealous and generous persons, are numerous and costly. They are valued at $1,800. The price of each window and the names of its donors are recorded as follows: Rose window, over sanctuary, $312, Married Ladies' Sodality; beautiful front window, $375 or $400, children of the parish; support window, beneath that of children, $45, nine of the oldest men of the congregation; window, $150, Holy Name Society. The ladies contributed liberally to the beautiful oil stations of the cross, valued at $600. The Young Ladies' Sodality bought the sanctuary lamp for $110. The statues of St. Joseph and the Blessed Virgin, valued at $200, were given by ten ladies of the congregation.

RECENT DONATIONS TO ST. MARY'S CHURCH.

In addition to the above, which refers to donations made when the church was first built, we will here mention the many gifts presented at various times since then. Individual married ladies gave the following costly objects: A statue of the Sacred Heart of Jesus, a statue of the Sacred Heart of Mary, a commodious, hard-wood vestment case; a marble and onyx credence table, for the sanctuary, and a gold plated chalice, used two hundred years ago in Ireland, by a Dominican priest. The credence table was presented by a young lady, in her mother's name, to be a memorial of that dear parent, when she shall have gone to her eternal reward. This manner of commemorating the beloved friends, who have departed this life, is eminently more touching than the erection of lofty monuments in the grave-yard.

Rich laces, beautiful altar linens, handsome albs and other valuable altar furnishings, were donated by the Married Ladies' Sodality.

A beautifully sculptured, white marble baptismal font, exquisitely ornamented, with carvings of graceful design, was presented by a gentleman and his wife. Another gentleman paid the entire cost of the Blessed Virgin's altar of marble and onyx, and a third, aided by his sister, did the same for the altar of St. Joseph, which is of the same costly material, and was given as a memorial of a beloved sister, at that time, recently deceased. This is another noble example for those of our parishioners who have means to erect expensive memorials to honor deceased relatives; let them glorify God at the same time.

A handsome, life size statue of St. Patrick was presented, soon after the erection of the church, by a gentleman who thereby mingled piety and patriotism. About the same time, the children of St. Mary's school donated the statue of St. Thomas Aquinas, their especial patron.

Among the early presentations made to the church was one of the most sacred and most valuable, an offering from twenty-five ladies. This is still in use, and is the exceedingly beautiful gold plated "Remonstrance" that holds so important a place in the Benediction service.

The large brazen crosses that were attached to the doors of the grand entrance, during the consecration ceremonies, were donated by the Young Ladies' Sodality and by the St. Thomas Sodality. The young ladies had previously given the eighteen brass candle sticks of Gothic design that ornament the three marble altars.

An exquisitely embroidered preaching stole was presented by eighteen young ladies of the parish, at the time of the Jubilee celebration. The gold plated wine cruets were also a present, and, on the same occasion, many costly personal gifts came to the reverend pastor of St. Mary's, from friends in Chicago, and in the East and South.

THE CORNER STONE.

The corner stone was laid on Sunday, August 3, 1890, at 5 o'clock. There were 3000 people present, including a large delegation from abroad, Rockford sending her full quota. The procession, headed by the Henney Buggy Company Band, included St. Joseph's Society, and St. Pius Society, of St. Joseph's Church, the Holy Name Society of St. Mary's Church, and the Ancient Order of Hibernians, of Rockford, in command of P. W. Welch, and the last named were accompanied by a drum corps.

The inscription on the stone is: "I say to thee that thou art Peter, and upon this rock I will build my church, and the gates of hell shall not prevail against it."—St. Matt. xvi : 18; A. D. 1890." The box enclosed in the stone contains city and other papers, coins, manuscript, etc. Father McLaughlin, of Rockford, made an eloquent address, at the conclusion of which Rev. Father Horan spoke a few words of thanks to the contractors, the architect and others, after which the exercises closed.

A GRAND EDIFICE.

The church, 53 x 137 feet, is built of stone quarried near Freeport, and the trimmings are terra cotta. It fronts on State street, and is placed near the north end of the lot, with the parochial house, 38x40 feet, about ninety feet from the front and attached to the church, leaving a pleasant lawn in the angle, with south and west exposure. The design of the church is modern Gothic. A tower, sixteen feet square at the base and 110 feet in height, caps the northeast corner of the main front, while a smaller tower graces the southwest corner. The larger one has been heavily and substantially built to receive a chime of bells at some future date.

The approach to the main entrance to the edifice is by three stone steps to a broad stone platform extending across the front from tower to tower. Two pairs of wide double doors, set in stone and surrounded by terra cotta, give entrance to a commodious

MR. AND MRS. P. O'CONNOR.
MR. AND MRS. JAMES FLANAGAN.
MRS. H. GLENNON.
MRS. J. RIORDAN.

vestibule, 10 x 30 feet. Above the main entrance, a row of entresol windows forms an imposing effect as the base of a large window. This window has a fine Gothic tracery and is filled with art glass in appropriate designs. The side walls of the structure are twenty feet in height with heavy buttresses between the windows. The height of the nave is thirty-five feet. The roof is covered with metallic shingles in Gothic pattern.

The main auditorium has 665 sittings, with broad six-foot aisle in the center, and two four-foot aisles, with seven feet between the front seat and altar rail.

Above the vestibule and extending three feet into the church, with handsomely curved panel-front, is the organ and choir loft, with appropriate furnishings.

The wood work throughout is of southern pine, finished in the natural graining of the wood. The ceiling is adorned with partially exposed trusses, and is handsomely frescoed. The artist was David Dasso, of Chicago. Back of and higher than the altar is a handsome rose window, containing a representation of the Immaculate Conception.

The main altar span is raised two steps above the floor of the nave and occupies 24 x 25 feet of space; the side altars, 7 x 18 feet. The pulpit, of different woods, is handsomely finished and durably constructed.

There is a large sacristy at the north of the main altar, and a robing room for the boys is on the south side. In the basement of the church there is a large winter chapel, also furnace rooms, coal rooms, etc.

The parochial house has two stories and a basement in height; it contains twenty-one rooms and four closets. In the basement there are two pantries, a dining room, a store room and wine vaults.

Owing to the grade of the lot, which slopes to Union Street, the basement rooms, both in the house and church, have pleasant open frontage.

The first floor of the parochial house has an ante-hall seven feet in width, separated from the foyer hall by a stairway; in the latter there is a handsome oak staircase, the balustrade of which contains 3,000 pieces. On the right of the hall is a reception room, an entrance to the church and a west chamber; on the left are two libraries. There is also the pastor's bedroom, and a closet on this floor. The windows in the east and west ends of these rooms are set in curved fronts.

The second floor has a library and living room over similar rooms on the first floor, with assistant priest's chamber, bath room, clothes closet, etc.

On the third story, there are four large rooms; one for a store room; another for a general room and two large bright rooms for the housekeeper.

The house, like the church, is built of stone, with terra cotta trimminngs. The entire expense of the church, when completed and furnished, was over $40,000.

For convenience in all its parts and good taste in all its appointments, it is not surpassed by any church, outside of Chicago. Well lighted with gas, comfortably heated with steam in winter and admirably ventilated in summer, worshipers find it free from distracting discomforts, and come to it as to a haven of rest and peace.

The parochial house adjoins the church, and communicates with it, by means of a vestry. It is comfortably, though not expensively furnished; all the pieces are of hard wood, upholstered with plush or with leather. The mantles are elegant and below them are fine fire-places, beautifully tiled, some of them containing gas logs which, when lit, on a chilly evening, give delightful warmth and "a dim religious light" provocative of reflection and meditation.

On the walls of the parlor are two pictures, highly prized by the pastor, to whom they were personally presented, one, of the Sacred Heart of Jesus, by the Sisters of Mercy of St. Xavier's Academy, Chicago, and the other, a life size portrait of Cardinal Gibbons, by the Dominican Sisters of Sinsinawa, Wis. Both are painted in oil and are the work of artists belonging to the communities that presented them.

The Cardinal sat especially for the portrait and considers it one of his best pictures.

Aside from its excellent furnishings, St. Mary's Rectory is one of the prettiest and pleasantest dwellings imaginable; there is not a dull, ill-lighted or, in any sense, unpleasant room to be found in it, from basement to garret.

The interior of the church is grandly furnished. The altars of marble and onyx are very beautiful; the walls are frescoed in water colors, the work of David Dasso of Chicago, and the aisles are matted. The sacristy memorial windows bear the names of: Revs. John Cavanaugh, Ferdinand Kalvalage, Thomas O'Gara, Thomas Kennedy, George Rigby, M. J. Hanley, T. L. Hendricks, F. J. Murtaugh, M. Stack, Thomas F. Mangan and M. Welby.

The plans for the new church were drawn by G. Stanley Mansfield, of Freeport, the architect, and being found perfectly satisfactory, by the committee who had the matter in charge, were accepted. Everything connected with the building of the new edifice has been creditable to the designer.

One of the very satisfactory features of the affairs of St. Mary's Church is the harmonious completeness with which every thing was arranged, from the very first. There has been no lack of proper and suitable altar furnishings, no shabby, half-worn vestments, no defects or deficiencies anywhere; everything essential to the ceremonial of the Catholic Church has been present, and all things have been new together.

The choir, which has an excellent name, for fine voices and good work, comprises the following young people: Miss Mary Brennan, organist; Mrs. Leo Thro, Miss Maggie Carey, Mrs. M. Ellsworth, sopranos; Miss Jennie P. Tracy, mezzo soprano; Miss Nonie Reardon, contralto; John P. Lawless, tenor; Edward Lawless, baritone; John Rau, Frank Rogers, bassos. J. E. Carroll, the able director, drills the choir and keeps it up to its high standard.

That there should have been a universal sentiment of joy among the parishioners, on the completion of the church, was quite natural, and it is needless to state that its dedication was a matter of special interest to each of them, for the occasion was one of personal as well as general satisfaction.

THE SOLEMN OPENING OF ST. MARY'S CATHOLIC CHURCH.

In the presence of a large number of clergymen and other friends and spectators, from home and abroad, the first solemn

SIDE VIEW OF ST. MARY'S CHURCH.

opening of St. Mary's new Catholic Church occurred on Wednesday, October 28, 1891.

It was the intention to dedicate the sacred edifice on this occasion, but in consequence of the illness of Archbishop Feehan, and the non-arrival of Bishop Cotter of Winona, Minn., whom the archbishop supposed to be present to act in his place, the dedication was necessarily deferred. The disappointment was greater than words can express, for every man, woman and child had been actively engaged in making grand preparations for the occasion, and all were generously interested in its success, towards which all had contributed both labor and money.

The Catholics of Freeport have every reason to be proud of the work accomplished by them in the year 1891, and Rev. W. A. Horan is to be congratulated on the grand success which, in union with his devoted people, he has achieved.

In one short year, he caused the erection of a church, also of a parochial residence, freeing both of them, in the same brief period, from every cent of debt. Nor is this all; the school house was enlarged and a beautiful hall, for public purposes, was constructed above the school rooms. Too much praise cannot be accorded the superlative energy that accomplished so much in so short a time. The expressions of appreciation and admiration that the speakers of the day lavished on the pastor of St. Mary's were richly merited by him and were music to the ears of his devoted flock.

At 10 o'clock, on the eventful day of the solemn opening of St. Mary's new church, an immense throng of parishioners and guests was present in the handsome edifice. The altars appeared even more beautiful than usual, plants and flowers being used in great quantities as decorations. The services throughout, were very impressive and in perfect keeping with the occasion. Rev. Father F. Kalvalege of St. Francis' Church, Chicago, the veteran clergyman, who was the second pastor of St. Mary's Church, was the celebrant of the Mass; Father White of Wisconsin, was the deacon; Father Flaherty of Rockford, sub-deacon; Father Byrne of Rockford, master of ceremonies. The sermon, which was eloquent and appropriate, was delivered by Rev. P. J. Muldoon, chancellor of the archdiocese of Chicago, a man of great ability, a brilliant orator and a zealous priest, who could not fail to be inspired by an occasion so entirely in accord with his own desires and aims.

The speaker based his remarks on the words "His house will be the house of prayer," and said: "No words can be too strong, too expressive, with which to thank the people for their generosity in giving this noble gift to God. It is, indeed worthy to be a house of prayer, emblematic of all that is good. What is prayer, but speech with God? And where may we so fittingly speak with Him, as in the temple erected to His honor, by a lively faith and supernatural charity? Then we must believe in some

REAR VIEW OF ST. MARY'S CHURCH AND RESIDENCE.

higher being, else we cannot have prayer, and not having prayer we would not need a house of worship. It is from God we receive all kindness and mercy; to Him we owe, for that reason, the unbounded thanks that will be offered unceasingly in this His temple.

"In the building and erection of every church there is shown a belief in God. It is not from earthly vanity that these temples are reared. We realize there is a God from whom we receive all blessings. Our hopes are not on the earth, for we have not our abiding city here. We understand that there is a home above, and it is for that reason that we give loud acclamations in tones of joy, when such temples are built. These buildings declare that there is a God and that we are held responsible for our deeds with regard to our neighbor and to our God. The erection of such a structure must be based on a desire to love and serve God.

"We are here to-day and away to-morrow. We must account for the things in our possession. We are to use our abilities for God. We cannot prepare for heaven in a moment. It is our duty and we are expected always to do good.

"I can say no words too strong in praise of the work of St. Mary's congregation. I do not say it with flattery, and I say it after having seen all the churches of the diocese, that there is none more beautiful than this. There may be some grander and larger, none are more complete, none more artistic. You have seen great changes in your parish in a year. The old church, which stood so many years, has been replaced by an edifice complete and furnished throughout.

"In olden times the people were not allowed to present anything to God that was defiled or imperfect. You seemed to have this object in view when you prepared your church to give to Him. You have brought it to Him without a blemish. Your work is wonderful, when you consider the size of the parish and the size of the city itself. It is always easy to build a church, but many times it is difficult to pay for it, when finished.

"When we see this people carry their gift to God, we call it wonderful. It shows love for Almighty God and it recalls visions of the olden time, when the people came bearing their most precious gifts. It is not the mechanic nor the designer who has done this, but the spirit which has opened the hearts in generosity. May you live long to enjoy the fruits of your labor.

"Some of you may have heard thirty years ago the same voice asking blessing upon the seed he had sown, that you hear to-day blessing the growth thereof.

"Here is where your children will receive their first blessing.

It is here that you will be carried on your journey to your last home.

"In all that has been done you should be thankful to God. Nobody can do much unless there is some guiding star. You have had your guiding star. He has led you to become an example of zeal to the people of the diocese. Pray for him, that he may be spared to you and may be led on to complete his great work.

AN INTERIOR VIEW OF ST. MARY'S PAROCHIAL RESIDENCE.

"God will return a hundredfold what you have given Him. With a church, home and school, you have all that goes to make up a great congregation and to fit your children to become true American citizens. In all this, love and thank Him, for no praise can be too much, in return for such favors."

Hayden's Imperial Mass was rendered by ladies and gentlemen of Chicago, Mr. Winder presiding at the organ. It was a magnificent treat in the church music line. Mrs. Dr. Hemmi rendered a soprano solo, "O Salutaris," Mr. A. E. Dasso gave the "Veni Creator" as a tenor solo, and Miss Coffee, Mrs. Hemmi and Mr. Dasso sang a trio.

After mass, all repaired to the new hall which had been handsomely decorated with flags, bunting and pictures. There at noon a banquet was given to the clergymen and others in attendance.

Great credit was given the ladies of St. Mary's Church, both young and old, for the magnificent spread they prepared, as well as for the beautiful arrangement of the tables and the elegant serving of the repast.

A number of toasts were proposed and happily responded to by several clergymen in attendance, who were loud in praise of Freeport and Freeporters.

The Chicago choir and the members of the home choir were entertained at the parochial residence.

The clergymen who were in attendance at the solemn opening were:—

Rev. Thos. F. Cashman, Chicago.
Rev. Daniel McGuire, Chicago.
Rev. F. W. Pape, New Vienna, Ia.
Rev. D. B. Toomey, Polo, Ill.
Rev. L. Erhard, Somonauk, Ill.
Rev. J. J. Flaherty, Rockford, Ill.
Rev. Stephen Woulfe, Rockford, Ill.
Rev. W. White, Hammond, Wis.
Rev. J. Nicholas, Elkhorn, Wis.
Rev. A. Beuter, Shannon, Ill.
Rev. H. M. Fegers, Sterling, Ill.
Rev. O'Connor, chancellor Peoria diocese, Peoria, Ill.
Rev. F. L. DuFour, Niagara, N. Y.

Rev. P. J. Muldoon, Chicago.
Rev. F. Kalvalege, Chicago.
Rev. J. E. Shanahan, Apple River.
Rev. M. Luby, Maytown, Ill.
Rev. A. O. Walker, Sinsinawa.
Rev. P. F. Byrne, Rockford, Ill.
Rev. A. J. Carroll, Rochelle, Ill.
Rev. G. Brady, Portage, Wis.
Rev. C. Hudt, Hampshire, Ill.
Rev. F. Antil, Savanna, Ill.
Rev. J. F. Power, Spring Valley, Ill.
Rev. Weldon, Bloomington, Ill.
Rev. Shannon, Brimfield, Ill.
Rev. C. Kalvalege, Freeport.

Michael Horan, father of Father Horan, Miss Horan, a sister, Michael and Thomas, brothers, all of DeKalb, and Stephen, another brother, of Rockford, were also in attendance.

Many letters of regret were received by Father Horan from all over the country. Bishop J. Shanley of Fargo, North Dakota, wrote as follows:

DEAR FATHER HORAN:—I cannot tell you my disappointment at being unable to be present at your church consecration Oct. 28th. Over a month ago I promised to begin a week's mission in Fairbault, Minn., on Oct. 25th. I have tried to change the time of the mission, but without success. Your good people and yourself deserve all honors for your wonderful work, and for that reason, as well as for my deep regard for yourself, I would wish to be with you on that great day. With best wishes,

Fraternally yours,

J. SHANLEY.

AN INTERIOR VIEW OF ST. MARY'S PAROCHIAL RESIDENCE.

His grace, Bishop M. F. Burke of the Cheyenne Diocese, writes from St. Mary's Cathedral under date of Oct. 21. He says:

DEAR FATHER HORAN:—I have been away from home at the Indian mission in the interior of the State for the past two weeks, and on my return I found awaiting me, your very kind letter of invitation to be present at your dedication, on the 28th inst. I thank you very much for your kindness and sincerely regret that it will be quite impossible for me to be with you on the happy occasion. I am engaged this week; next week will be all alone and could not possibly get away even if the distance were not so great. Trusting to have the pleasure of visiting you on some other occasion, and wishing that you may be long spared to your good and generous people to enjoy your beautiful church, I am with great respect,

Very kindly yours,
M. F. BURKE.

A sacred concert was given at St. Mary's Church after the opening ceremonies and was in all respects worthy of the ladies and gentlemen from Chicago who participated, and highly appreciated by the very large audience that had assembled. There were present many of Freeport's representative citizens, and none but words of praise were heard regarding the efforts of those who were on the program.

The first number was the gloria from Mozart's 12th Mass, given with fine effect and in good chorus by the choir. This was followed by an alto solo, "Dreams," by Streliski, rendered by Miss Frances McCaffrey, a lady who has a beautiful voice that she knows well how to use. Later in the evening, she sang a selection from Handel's Messiah, "He was despised and rejected," displaying to good advantage the remarkable strength of her voice. Agustin E. Dasso, who belongs to the choir of St. Patrick's Church, sang "Cujus Animam," by Rossini, in a clear and high tenor voice, and in a highly acceptable manner; this was followed by a solo, "Aria Attilla," given by Mrs. Dr. S. Hemmi, in a soprano voice of wide range, cultivation and sweetness. She quite captivated the audience. "Inflammatus," by Rossini, was a soprano solo and chorus that made a good impression, Mrs. E. G. Stevenson taking the solo part. This was followed by a bass solo, "Pro Peccatis," F. A. Langlois singing for the first time in Freeport. This gentleman is a member of the cathedral quartette and it is always a pleasure to hear him, for he is a favorite everywhere. Mr. Langlois and Charles Moore, the well known tenor of St. Mary's, Chicago, sang "O Salutaris," by Verdi, in a manner that was highly appreciated. Carl Bernhard, the baritone soloist of St. James', was also with the party, and his rendering of "The Jewess" evinced talent of high order. The trio "Te

Prego O Padre," gave ample scope for the excellent voices of Mrs. Hemmi, A. E. Dasso and F. A. Langlois. The last number on the program, "Good Night," was the finale to a concert that was richly enjoyed by every one whose good fortune it was to attend. Should these ladies and gentlemen appear in a concert in Freeport again, it is certain they will be warmly welcomed.

G. STANLEY MANSFIELD,
Architect of St. Mary's New Church and Parochial Residence.

John H. Winder, the organist of St. Patrick's church, Chicago, a gentleman eminent in his profession, played the accompaniments on the pipe organ. David Dasso made the arrangements for the concert, and his efforts were sincerely appreciated by the people of St. Mary's and by other interested citizens.

ST. MARY'S HALL AND ST. MARY'S SCHOOL BUILDING.

Next to the church, Father Horan and his people hold the school to be the most precious possession of the congregation. To its progress the pastor has ever devoted an untiring energy and an unceasing vigilance. Hence there was no surprise when, in the spring of 1891, he announced that a new school building, with a hall for public purposes, would be erected during the summer, and that the expense would be met with the proceeds of entertainments, lectures and concerts. The work was immediately begun and energetically pushed forward.

The hall was built under the direction of the following committee: J. P. Younger, president; John E. Hogan, secretary; F. Chas. Donohue, treasurer; Charles McNamara, John M. Peck, Martin Flanagan, James O'Rourke, Patrick Reedy, John J. Sweeney.

The contracts for the construction of the building were made with R. D. Dirksen, carpenter work; E. Bamberger, mill work; M. Scanlan, plastering; Kruze & Metzgar, brick; Bongye & Schwartz, painting and glazing; Wm. Ascher, stone work; Freeport Water Co., steam heating.

The structure is of brick and stone, two stories and a half high, and 54 x 104 feet in dimensions. The first floor comprises four school rooms, two class rooms and a library. On the second floor is the hall referred to above. A movable partition enables the Columbus Club to separate their part of this extensive auditorium from that devoted to entertainments, but on a great occasion, when the audience is likely to be large, this barrier is removed.

Heated by steam, lighted by electricity, and admirably ventilated, St. Mary's Hall, with a seating capacity of six hundred, can be adapted, by removing the chairs, to any parish purpose required. Within its walls, since it was first opened, on the evening of Thanksgiving day, in '91, there have been school exhibitions, dramatic entertainments, lectures and concerts, parties and bazaars. It has saved the parish hundreds of dollars of hall rent, always exorbitant, and has indirectly brought to the congregation a handsome profit, for many an honorable money-making scheme has been carried out, with marked success, that could never have been undertaken had there been no St. Mary's Hall. To sell a hundred dollars' worth of tickets is a profitable matter, when there is no hall rent to pay; not so, when at least forty dollars of the hundred must be given

ST. MARY'S SCHOOL AND HALL.

for the use of a hall, inconvenient, perhaps, as well as unsuitable.

The corner-stone of St. Mary's Hall was laid on Sunday, July 19, 1891, at 5 p. m., amid a large concourse of people, who listened with eager attention, to the eloquent and thoughtful address of Rev. E. J. Dunne, since consecrated Bishop of Dallas, Texas. The stone bears the inscription "Religion, Science, Peace, 1891," and encloses a box containing papers, coins, and other objects indicative of the laws and customs of our age.

Hon. Wm. Onahan of Chicago, addressed an immense audience, on the occasion of the opening of the hall, and he but headed the procession, as it were, of distinguished men who have, at short intervals, in the past five years, presented, for the consideration of St. Mary's people, their noblest sentiments, delivered in their best style.

John Lawless and Leo Thro were appointed stage managers, and all entertainments presented in the new hall, were conducted under their direction.

A series of enjoyable social events occurred during the winter that followed the opening of the hall, and both dramatic and literary programs were presented, "The Shamrock and the Rose" being particularly successful, as was also a varied entertainment given by the Young Ladies' Literary Association. The pupils of St. Mary's school, likewise, afforded pleasure by the frequent presentation of interesting and original programs.

The hall is, in fact, admirably adapted to the presentation of dramatic entertainments. The stage is wide and deep, and brilliantly illuminated with electrical border-lights and foot-lights. The several sets of scenery, parlor, prison, forest and landscape, are easily arranged and give suitable environment for almost any sort of drama. The drop curtain, which represents the origin of the "Star Spangled Banner," was painted by David Dasso, a gifted Catholic citizen of Chicago. It presents a picture of the Bay of Baltimore, with Fort McHenry, and its battered flag, in the distance; the waves are lapping against the sides of a noble ship, a British man-of-war, on the deck of which stands Francis Key, the author of our national song, in the midst of a group of British tars. He has been captured and brought on board, where in the "dawn's early light," he beholds the star spangled banner, begrimmed indeed, but proudly floating over the fort. This he is triumphantly saluting, with hand and voice. At the top and left side of the picture appears a mammoth flag, gracefully draped, while at the right there stands a large vase of flowers. The curtain as a whole, is very pretty and effective.

During the winter season, there is a social gathering of Catholic citizens in St. Mary's hall, every two weeks, except, of course, in Advent and in Lent. A musical program is followed by dancing and refreshments. Thus are Catholic young people brought together, instead of being left to wander about among those not in religious sympathy with them, and therefore likely to be dangerous companions.

The first school connected with St. Mary's Church was in existence during the time of Father Kalvalege's pastorate. It was

MR. AND MRS. P. H. MURPHY.

intended, principally for the German portion of the congregation and was discontinued soon after being established. The next effort to institute a school was made in the time of Rev. T. J. Murtaugh who, with the assistance of ex-Ald. A. J. McCoy and others, raised money and purchased the two story brick building which is still standing, and forms a part of the new school house and hall. The lot adjoining was also purchased, thus enlarging the grounds. The building was found to be well suited for school purposes, and capable of accommodating two hundred and fifty pupils. It was Father Stack who went to the Mother House of the Dominican order at Sinsinawa Mound and secured the number of Sisters necessary to conduct the new school, which opened in August, 1873.

The Order of Dominican Sisters was established six hundred years ago, by St. Dominic, a Spanish nobleman of great sanctity and wisdom. His Order, both of priests and nuns, has given many saints to the church, and was approved and confirmed by the learned Popes, Gregory IX., Boniface IX., Innocent VII., and Eugene IV. The object of the Third Order of Dominican Nuns is to provide religious instruction for girls living in the world and exposed to its trials and temptations. From Spain, the Order spread rapidly through Italy, France, and other parts of Europe. About 1812, it was established in Ohio and Kentucky, and, a few years later, in Wisconsin. For a year before and a year after receiving the religious habit, the noble women belonging to this Order remain in the training school, at the Mother House, Sinsinawa, Wis., preparing for their important duties as religious teachers, duties demanding the acquirements of the best secular teachers and, in addition to them, the ability to give religious instruction by word and example.

St. Clara's Academy supplies teachers for schools in thirty cities, the farthest west being Denver and the farthest south Washington, D. C. The Dominican Sisters are widely spread in the United States and have several Mother Houses, each with its many branch houses. It was at Memphis, during the raging of the yellow fever, that Dominican Sisters left their schools to help care for the sick; many of them never returned to their schools, because the dread disease which they might easily have escaped, gave them a martyr's death. The services of Sisters of this Order have been long devoted to St. Mary's precious heritage, the little ones of the flock, two hundred and fifty being the average enrollment of pupils.

The school is free and well graded. The pupils are classed in four departments, viz.: Primary, having four grades and two teachers; the Intermediate, having two grades and one teacher; the Grammar Department, four grades and two teachers; the High School Department, two grades and one teacher.

ST. MARY'S SCHOOL.

The text books and the course of study are the same as used in the public schools of the city, but half an hour is daily devoted to instructions in Christian Doctrine.

Three grades of honors are conferred on the occasion of the annual commencement of St. Mary's School: first, the laurel crowns, given to those who have been examined by the county superintendent, and have received from him a second grade certificate; second, diplomas, conferred on those who have been examined by the county superintendent in the additional studies required for a first grade certificate, and have attained the average required for graduation from the city High School; third, a gold medal, conferred on graduates whose deportment has been exemplary in all particulars.

Each year, since Father Horan has required the members of grades eleven and twelve, both boys and girls, to take the "teachers' examination," at the court house, under direction of the county superintendent, there have been from two to eight of St. Mary's High School pupils, not above eighteen years of age, successful in gaining second grade certificates, and an excellent standing for the first grade. A first grade certificate is conferred only after the applicant has taught for a certain time.

Instrumental and vocal music receive careful attention. The pupils of the school are given lessons daily in singing by note. Special attention is given to literature, interest being aroused and preserved by duly organized reading circles, of which there are three, namely, "The Feehan Circle" comprising the high school pupils, "The Bryant-Whittier," to which belong the girls of the grammar department, and "The Longfellow," consisting of the boys of the same department. The ladies of the parish, a chosen few of them, are banded under the title of "The Aquinata Reading Circle," and since the above were established the higher grades in the primary department have united under the title of "The Father Horan Reading Circle."

The Young Ladies' Sodality has a fine library of nearly four hundred volumes. Many of those were donated by the pastor; others were obtained by means of entertainments.

Several volumes in the Sodality library being considered rather childish for such a collection, the young ladies donated them to the school library in the grammar department.

ST. MARY'S CONVENT.

"The Longfellow Circle" collected, during the first year of their association, over eighty volumes. These were donated by non-Catholics as well as Catholics, so agreeable is the spirit that governs the social relations of Freeport's citizens.

The school children edit a monthly journal, the "Santa Maria," and the profits it brings in are devoted to the purchase of books and periodicals. This little monthly edited by the children, whose compositions constitute its literature, has been ranked by competent critics, with the best college journals. That St. Mary's pupils are earnest parishioners in other particulars is proven by the following facts.

When the new church was in the process of erection, the children of St. Mary's school were as interested as their parents in all that concerned it, and they wanted to do something to help

CHARLES DUBS,
JOE G. ALLEN.
LIZZIE F. CORCORAN.
KITTIE KILLION.
JOHN MANION,
JOHN FLANAGAN.

EDITORS AND MANAGERS OF THE SANTA MARIA FOR 1896.

on the good work. Their teachers suggested having a bank in which the pupils could place their donations. These were to be the fruit of self-sacrifice; money given the children by their parents to spend on sweet meats was dropped into the bank instead, and, when the pennies and nickels amounted to many dollars, the sum was devoted to the purchase of a magnificent stained window representing the Holy Family. This beautiful donation has a place of honor over the front entrance, and bears an inscription stating that the little ones of the flock contributed this handsome addition to the very beautiful and costly set of windows that adorn St. Mary's Church.

A PAGE FROM FATHER HORAN'S LIFE.

Here we think it well to give a brief biographical sketch of him, to whom, under God, all this success, so honorable to religion, is due.

His life has been crowded with zealous activity and crowned with remarkable success. Rev. W. A. Horan, pastor of St. Mary's Church, is a son of Patrick and Mary (Hanaughan) Horan, and was born at DeKalb, Ill., Feb. 2, 1851. His father was, for some years, a dry goods merchant in Chicago; this he abandoned to engage in farming at DeKalb, Ill. There were eight children in the family. William, upon attaining the proper age, was enrolled in the public school, near his home, where he pursued his studies, with marked interest and earnestness. His aptitude in pursuing the branches of a higher course, is apparent, when it is learned that he graduated from the high school, with honor, at the age of fifteen.

Having decided to fit himself for the priesthood, he went to that celebrated institute of learning, the University of Niagara, New York, at which place he spent ten years, six in classical studies and four in theology. He finished the university course in 1877, and on May 26th of the same year, was ordained to the priesthood, by Bishop Ryan of Buffalo, N. Y.

The training of a Catholic priest is very exacting, and requires many years of the hardest kind of mental exertion. The fact that Father Horan completed his studies and was ordained a priest at the early age of twenty-five, shows that he was possessed not only of unusually fine abilities, but also of the spirit of determination and of habits of application.

His first mission was at St. James' Catholic Church, Chicago, under Father P. W. Reardon, the present Archbishop of San Francisco, Cal. Here he remained from 1877 to 1879. His abilities becoming recognized, he was assigned to duty at the Cook County hospital, a position not only teeming with opportunities for doing good, but also, attended by lurking dangers that threaten the ruin of the strongest constitution. He resided with Rev. Thomas F. Cashman, assisting him in his manifold duties. It was a life of busy activity for the youthful priest, and, though the time spent amid the foul air of the hospital had impressed its biting seal upon his robust constitution, he would not have had those years spent otherwise, for he considers the difficult duties there fulfilled to have been the greatest work of his life. He was engaged almost incessantly in attending the sick, smoothing the pillow of the dying, and in performing the last offices for the dead. From the lips of the sufferers he learned many of life's experiences that awoke his interest and sympathy, and brought him in close relation with people from various and even distant parts of our country, for, in the great city of Chicago it is strangers, persons from other parts of the United States, who are carried to the hospital, in case of accidents or sickness. Within its walls are found many people who have no homes, and others whose homes are too distant to admit the patient's removal to them. Much to his regret, Father Horan was obliged to give up his work at the hospital, and, in 1882, he was appointed pastor of St. Thomas' Church, Hyde Park. The parish then included not only Hyde Park, but also Auburn. While stationed there he raised funds and erected St. Lawrence Church at Grand Crossing, St. Leo's Church at Auburn, and began the new church of St. Thomas at Hyde Park. A fine parochial house in connection with the latter was erected, besides the school building and a convent for the Sisters. One hundred feet of ground had been purchased, and the walls of the church had been erected, when Father Horan was obliged to relinquish his work and travel for the benefit of his health. The vicinity of the lake had a tendency to aggravate his disease, which continued to grow worse, until

REV. FATHER HORAN.

the patient was compelled to seek other climes. By advice of Dr. Murphy, and other prominent physicians of Chicago, he spent the winters of 1887 and 1888 in the south, much of his time being occupied in New Orleans, La., and Jacksonville and Pensacola, Fla.

In the summer of 1888 he went to Minnesota, and part of the next winter was spent in Chicago, after which he enjoyed a trip to Denver and Salt Lake City in company with his warm friends, Judge Pendergast, of Chicago, and Father White, of Wisconsin. The next fall he arranged to go south after the holidays, but was requested to proceed to Freeport to take charge of St. Mary's congregation during the absence of Father Welby. The death of the latter, while in Mexico, created a vacancy in St. Mary's parish. When it became necessary to appoint a successor to the deceased pastor, it was not strange that universal sentiment was in favor of the young priest who was in temporary charge of the congregation; he had so greatly endeared himself to the people that they were unwilling to part with him, and petitioned the Archbishop of Chicago to appoint him to the vacant pastorate. It was a happy day for all concerned when he was assigned permanently to Freeport.

Since then he has worked indefatigably for his people. No sacrifice has been too great, no effort too mighty for him to make in their behalf. He has given them a magnificent parochial residence and a commodius hall and school, besides the handsome church.

Father Horan has also been benefited by his appointment, for during his sojourn in Freeport, he has improved wonderfully in health. The sick spells that were frequent, when he first came here, occur but seldom, and, he appears to grow stronger with each dawning day. He has done a world of good, and has won the everlasting love and gratitude of every member of his church and every child in the parish.

The father of Rev. W. A. Horan is still living and is a hale and hearty gentleman 93 years old. One brother is in the real estate and dry goods business at DeKalb, Ill., one is farming, and the youngest, Stephen, is a druggist at Rockford. Only one of his sisters is living, she was present on the occasion of the dedication. Another was a sister of Charity, Sister St. Vincent, who died some years ago at the Mother's House at Emmetsburg, Va. Father Horan's mother and Cardinal Gibbons were first cousins.

REV. FATHER DU FOUR.

Rev. Father Du Four, who came to Freeport to assist Father Horan, had but recently arrived, at the time of the dedication, but has participated enthusiastically in all parish affairs since

REV. FATHER DU FOUR.

that occasion. He is noted for his eloquence as a pulpit speaker, for his culture and his wide range of information. A native of St. Genevive, Mo., his earliest recollections are of St. Louis, where he was a student during his youth. There he attended the

Christian Brothers' school, and later went to the institute at Cape Girardeau. In 1878 he entered the well-known St. Vincent's Seminary at Germantown, Pa., and afterwards returned to Cape Girardeau as an instructor, where, in 1882, he was ordained to the priesthood. For several years he was connected with the celebrated Niagara University as professor of mathematics, came west a short time since, and will doubtless not return to the east. He has occupied St. Mary's pulpit frequently, and his discourses have been listened to with a great deal of pleasure and satisfaction.

THE RECORD OF ST. JOSEPH'S CHURCH.

It is fitting that we here introduce to our readers St. Mary's noble sister-church, St. Joseph's, a handsome edifice erected and used by an eminently pious and respectable German congregation, organized thirty years ago.

As we have elsewhere stated, in the early times the German and the Irish Catholics were members of one congregation, but many of the former being ignorant of the English language, it was deemed advisable to form two parishes. Father John Westkamp set about selecting a suitable place of worship for the Germans, and, on June 4, 1862, purchased the old Baptist Church, on the present site, for $2,000. The congregation at that time numbered 125 families. This old church was repaired and fitted up in good style, but in 1868, finding that it was too small to hold the rapidly growing congregation, a large gallery was built in it, and in the fall of 1871 it was decided to erect a new building. During the winter, the members living in the city quarried stone and the farming class hauled it to the site for the new edifice. Early in the spring, the old building was moved back to Pleasant Street and used for church purposes until the new structure was completed, after which it was torn down, and the lumber sold. The new church was immediately commenced.

The contracts were let as follows: Carpenter work, Straub & Baumgarten; brick, L. Metzgar; mason, Shoeb & Bruehler; plastering, Heitzman & Snyder; frescoing, D. Adamson.

Early in June the corner stone was laid by Bishop Foley, of Chicago, in the midst of a large number of priests and people. It was completed in December, 1872, and dedicated on the fourth Sunday of Advent by Bishop Foley, in the presence of a great many priests from all parts of the diocese.

REV. FATHER KALVELAGE.

The building is of modern Gothic, its dimensions are 50 x 140 feet, and the cost was $35,000. The church is built of brick with stone trimmings and faces northeast. John Dillenburg, of Chicago, was the architect. The seating capacity including the gallery is 850. It is lighted with gas and heated by means of large furnaces. The windows are of stained glass.

In 1881 the appearance of the sacred structure was greatly improved by the erection of the steeple, which is 175 feet high, and is of beautiful design and finish. Four bells, weighing 5,000 lbs. and costing $1,000, constitute a set of chimes that ring out joyously and solemnly on all religious feast days and on every Sunday. Their tones are E, F sharp, G sharp and A. They were purchased and hung during the pastorate of Father Kalvelage. In 1886 new altars were put into the church, at a cost of about $1,500. They were consecrated by Archbishop Feehan, May 20, 1886. The lower part has three reliefs, representing the marriage of the Blessed Virgin to St. Joseph; the nativity of our Lord, and the death of St. Joseph. There are three niches in the substructure. The larger one contains the crucifixion group, Christ on the cross and Mary and John beneath. In the right niche is the statue of the Immaculate Conception, and on the left, the statue of St. Boniface.

It was during the same year that the side altars and pews were purchased and put in. The interior furnishing and decorating are complete and choice, and St. Joseph's Catholic Church, from basement to steeple, is a structure of which our German citizens may well be proud.

Scarcely had the new church been completed and paid for, when efforts were made to improve the educational advantages. At first a small frame building, which had been purchased of St. Mary's congregation, and which stood on the present site, was used, but this became too small and was unsuited for the purpose, hence, in 1883, the new structure was begun.

The contracts were let as follows: Brick, John Trunck; stone, Bruchler & Eberle Bros.; carpenter work and plastering, D. Weary. F. E. Josel was the architect.

The building is fifty feet square. It has two stories and a basement, and is built of brick and stone. There are four school rooms, each 24 x 36 feet, with 12 foot ceilings. The basement is divided into a coal room and a room used for the various societies

connected with the church. The cost of the building was $5,500.
The school is divided into eight grades, there being four rooms of two grades each. Father Kalvelage superintends the

ST. JOSEPH'S CHURCH.

school and teaches catechism. The enrollment of pupils is 250, and the attendance is very regular, absence being occasioned only by sickness. Father Kalvelage has been very earnest in his efforts to improve the school, and bring it up to a high standard of scholarship and thoroughness. The parishioners very highly appreciate the excellent work done in St. Joseph's School. It is taught by Franciscan Sisters from Joliet.

The congregation of St. Joseph's Catholic Church have left nothing undone that might tend to make them better men and women in all directions; they have established a number of societies for social and benevolent purposes, each of which has been doing a grand work for God and for souls. Father Kalvelage has directed and assisted very materially in the formation of these societies, and it is due to his assistance and the deep interest taken by the members, that each one has made such progress, financially and numerically.

St. Joseph's Benevolent Society was organized March 4, 1866, by Rev. Father Baluff. Its purpose is insurance, which ranges from $500 to $1,000. A sick-benefit of $4 per week is paid. The membership is sixty. Meetings are held on the last Sunday of each month.

The St. Pius Benevolent Society was formed June 20, 1880, by the young men, and its insurance and sick-benefits are the same as in the St. Joseph Society. Both organizations belong to the German Catholic Central Society. They meet on the third Sunday of each month. The membership is seventy.

St. George's Branch of the Catholic Knights of Illinois was organized a few years ago. It furnishes insurance $1,000 to $2,000. Its membership is thirty-five, and meetings are held on the first Sunday of the month.

St. Mary's Society originated Oct. 30, 1867. The object is to assist in getting ornaments for the church. Rev. Father Kalvelage is the director.

St. Cecilia's Society, which began Aug. 10, 1870, is composed of the young ladies of the parish, who assist in decorating the church, and in maintaining a circulating library. There are forty-five members.

St. Aloysius Society, for boys between the ages of twelve and eighteen years, dates from Jan. 18, 1891. The membership is twenty. They also have a sick-benefit.

ST. JOSEPH'S SCHOOL.

St. Agnes Society for girls was established March 31, 1891, and numbers thirty members. They assist in decorating the church and keeping up the library. One of the Sisters acts as president.

The admirable progress of St. Joseph's German Catholic Church has been due to the good work done by her pastors.

INTERIOR OF ST. JOSEPH'S SCHOOL.

They have left monuments of devotion and zeal that make brief sketches of their lives worthy of perusal.

Father John Westkamp was the first pastor. He was born in Westphalia, Germany. In his youth he came to America, and studied at the St. Vincent College, at Beatty, Pa. He was ordained at Chicago. His pastorate here continued until 1863, and it was during his charge that the congregation was organized and the first church property purchased.

Father Ignatius Baluff was born in Europe. He emigrated to America in his younger days, and studied at St. Vincent's College. His course was finished in Chicago, where he was ordained. He served as pastor from June, 1863, to January, 1874. The new church was built under his direction, and the parsonage, a substantial and commodious brick building, was purchased. The cemetery, containing four acres, was also secured during his pastorate.

FATHER CLEMENT KALVELAGE.

Father Kalvelage, the present pastor, was born at Lohne, Germany, Nov. 23, 1845. He is a son of Herman and Mary (Dekmann) Kalvelage. His father was a weaver by trade. He attended a Catholic school near his home until thirteen years old. On Oct. 20, 1858, he reached this country with his mother, his father having died when he was but a mere child. They went to Milwaukee, Wis., and there for five years he studied at the St. Francis Seminary. At the end of that time, four years were occupied in study in St. Mary's of the Lake, Chicago. Then another year was spent in study at Milwaukee, and on Jan. 29, 1869, he was ordained at Milwaukee by Archbishop Henni.

His first pastorate was at the St. Francis Church, Ottawa, where he remained five years. He took charge of the congregation in Freeport, March 11, 1874, of which he has since been the pastor, doing a world of good. During this time the new school house was built, the steeple erected, the bells purchased and the hospital built. He has officiated at 1,000 baptisms and performed 300 marriage ceremonies as pastor of St. Joseph's Church.

The financial condition of the church is very good. The debt on the church and school is paid. The property, not including the hospital, is valued at $60,000. The remaining debt on the hospital is $8,800. The congregation held a jubilee in 1887, celebrating their twenty-fifth anniversary.

REV. FR. MEYER.

The assistant pastor of St. Joseph's Church, Rev. Father Meyer, is a man who has rendered efficient service to Father Kalvelage since he came here, a few years ago. He is a man of fine attainments, an excellent pulpit orator, and a priest who is devoted to his calling, and he is a prime favorite with the members of the large congregation.

THE ST. FRANCIS HOSPITAL.

AN INSTITUTION OF WHICH FREEPORT IS PROUD—A NOBLE WORK.

Connected with St. Joseph's Catholic Church is the St. Francis Hospital, an institution of which all Freeport is proud. And it has already done a noble work, which cannot be estimated by dollars and cents, but rather computed in that great city above, where the treasures are much more precious than gems or gold.

It was through the efforts of Father Kalvelage that the hospital was erected and fitted up. The story of the Stoneman bequest is familiar to all our readers and need not be recounted. We have referred to the good work done by the building committees and the members of the congregation, in helping the project in various ways. The building was begun on a beautiful, commanding site, on South Walnut Street, in the year 1889.

It is a handsome brick, tastily planned and substantially built. The cost was $20,000, to which was added $10,000 for furnishing, bedding, etc. The building is 44 x 104 feet; it is three stories high with an eight foot basement. The interior is lighted with gas and has water in all rooms where necessary. Large steam boilers heat the rooms and ventilators and dust shafts are ranged throughout the building. A fine feature is the large porch on the east side, where convalescents may greet the rising sun, and draw hope and strength from its genial beams. The building was dedicated Feb. 12, 1890.

Everything, from basement to dome, is kept exquisitely neat, and the good Franciscan Sisters in charge are untiring in

ST. FRANCIS HOSPITAL.

their efforts in ministering to those under their charge. One room is set apart for old soldiers who may be ill, and the John A. Davis Post, G. A. R., have fitted it up in an appropriate style, which any old soldier would most certainly appreciate. Not only have a great many patients of this city been taken care of at the hospital, but also a number of traveling men, and the inhabitants of the surrounding country and towns have added to the roll of patients.

The hospital is sustained partly by a moderate charge and partly by the charitable contributions of friends and benefactors. The first annual report of this noble institution furnishes some interesting data. For instance, we find that the religious beliefs of the sixty-eight patients were as follows: Catholics, 28; Protestants, denomination not given, 25; Lutherans, 4; Episcopalians, 2; Shaker, 1; Methodists, 3; Presbyterians, 1; Evangelical, 1; Congregational, 1; no religion, 2. It would seem, from these statistics, that a greater number of non-Catholics than of Catholics have profited by this excellent institution, which owes its existence and continuance to Catholic charity and enterprise.

Golden Jubilee Celebration and Solemn Consecration of St. Mary's Church.

Only a reflective mind, inspired by a lively faith and a fervent piety, can appreciate fully the grand significance of a Golden Jubilee Celebration. Whether it be for an individual or a parish, it is an occasion of great joy in heaven, as well as on earth. Fortunately for the success of St. Mary's celebration, her people are capable of understanding the importance of such an event and were generous in giving to every plan their hearty support and perfect sympathy.

Early in September, arrangements were completed to carry out a programme, which for interest and magnificence could not be surpassed, even in cities of greater importance than Freeport.

The grandeur of the ceremonies and the exalted dignity of the officiating ecclesiastics contributed to the imposing character of the occasion and made a deep impression upon all the citizens, irrespective of creed, who assisted in honoring the event thus recalled.

The celebration of the golden jubilee anniversary of the establishment of Catholicity in Stephenson County took place on the 12th, 13th, 14th and 15th of September, 1896, the congregations of St. Mary's and of St. Joseph's Churches uniting to render everything as impresssive as possible. St. Mary's being the first church in the county to have a resident pastor, he was appointed by the Bishop of Chicago, in 1846, naturally, it became the centre of interest during the celebration, and next to it ranked St. Joseph's, since in the early days both congregations had attended service in the same church.

Rev. W. A. Horan, pastor of St. Mary's, took a very active part in the preparations for the jubilee, and for nearly a year previous to the great event he worked almost incessantly at his plans for its fitting celebration. Certainly the four days mentioned above will be red-letter days henceforth in the memory of St. Mary's people, and the events that distinguish them will still form part of the traditions of the city, as well as of the parish, when another century shall have passed away.

Special excursion trains brought great numbers of guests from various towns in Wisconsin and Illinois. The array of the church dignitaries in attendance was most impressive and encouraging, delighting the people, as giving a proof of the high esteem in which their beloved pastor is held by his ecclesiastical superiors and *confreres*.

September 12th was a busy day; everyone belonging to a committee was rushing about with pleased activity, worthy of the good cause, and Saturday evening found everything in admirable order for the opening of the celebration on Sunday morning.

Certain remote preparations, full of mystical meaning, had been made for the important ceremony of consecration. Among others was the erection of the twelve brazen crosses that distinguish consecrated churches. Symbolical of the twelve apostles, the foundation upon which rests the See of Rome, similar crosses are fixed upon the walls of but one church in the archdiocese and that is St. James' of Chicago, of which the distinguished Rev. Hugh McGuire is pastor. There are two prerequisites of consecration: the church must be entirely free from debt and built of stone or other lasting material. When once consecrated, the building stands forever as a holy place, until dismantled beyond recognition. The magnificence and pomp of the ceremonial of consecration are as splendid as the great resources of the most powerful ecclesiastical organization can make them. The clergymen and the church are dressed in their richest vestments, and

TRIUMPHAL ARCH IN FRONT OF ST. MARY'S CHURCH.

as a prelude, the archbishop, with his mitre, bearing his crosier, followed by a train of lesser dignitaries and priests, marches solemnly three times around the church. At the completion of each circuit of the building, he raps on the door of the church with the crosier, and the third time enters with his attendants. Within, a cross of ashes is strewn upon the floor, in which the archbishop marks with his staff of office the Greek and Latin alphabets, the languages of the church. The four walls are then annointed with holy oil, and the sign of the cross made on each, and then, one by one, the twelve brazen crosses are affixed with attendant ceremonies.

On the outside of each of the two doors of the main entrance to the church, a large brazen cross was also fastened during the ceremonies of consecration. These crosses were purchased and donated, in advance, by the Young Ladies' Sodality of the Blessed Virgin and the School Children's Sodality of St. Thomas.

The nave of the church was decorated with drapery and festooning of yellow and white, the effect being that of a sunburst. The organ loft was trimmed with the same colors, which swathed the rail, and depending were over-lapping festoons that hung in graceful folds. On account of the consecration ceremonies, no flowers could be used on the altars, the only dressings being the altar cloths of white waxed linen. During the services on Monday, masses of flowers gave color to the scene, and their perfume blended with that of the incense. The sanctuary was left severely simple in its adornments, since cheap decorations could only detract from the beauty of the costly altars of marble and onyx.

A great deal of activity was shown in and around St. Mary's Church and Hall, preparatory to the solemn services that were held there on Monday and Tuesday, in connection with the golden jubilee celebration. The work going forward, so far as it could be seen, was that of arranging the decorations, but there was much more in progress than was visible, the ladies' committee being particularly active in arranging for their share of the program.

INTERIOR OF ST. MARY'S CHURCH.

The lunch, lemonade and badge counters were erected under green bowers, in the school yard, and the three committees in charge of them exercised much energy and good taste in their decoration, so that by Saturday evening they presented so pleasing an appearance as to tempt customers, even before there was anything to buy. A heavy rain, that continued until about six or seven o'clock Sunday morning, somewhat impaired the beauty of the booths, but did not dampen the ardor of the ladies in charge of them, for they instituted, and continued, until the close of the jubilee, a brisk sale of badges, cigars and refreshments, the proceeds being designed for pious and charitable purposes.

The part of St. Mary's Hall that is used by the Columbus Club was most elaborately and tastefully decorated, in patriotic and religious designs and colors. This really artistic work was done under the direction of Mr. Leo Thro, who has a genius for such decoration.

The dramatic part of the hall was in readiness for the children's reception; the stage was decorated at the expense of the Feehan Reading Circle.

The banqueting hall was a scene of beauty, a joy forever, a delight to the feminine heart, and a surprise, no doubt, to the reverend masculine eyes that beheld it, in all the glory of its graceful drapery of damask and lace; its tasteful decorations, in papal and in union colors; its gleaming silver and glittering china; its flower decked tables groaning under their loads of viands. The jubilee dinner was a triumph of Freeport housekeeping, and Chicago caterers were left in the shade.

In an adjoining hall, of smaller size, a fine dinner was spread for the members of the Madison Band, which had been engaged, at a high price, to "discourse sweet music" on the street, before the church, in the hall during the banquet, and at intervals during the reception.

The climax of beauty was reached, however, in the triumphal arch that spanned State Street, in front of St. Mary's Church. About fifty feet high, double in construction, a space six feet in width between the two parts, and terminating at the top in points

INTERIOR OF ST. JOSEPH'S CHURCH.

and spires, as required by the gothic style of its design, the frame work was the support of gracefully arranged drapery in papal and union colors, of pictures of the reigning pope and of the present archbishop, of flags, garlands and three hundred incandescent lights. Many of these lights were arranged on a large cross that crowned the summit of the arch. The sacred symbol thus outlined, in vivid electric light, against a starlit sky, was one of the most striking features in the rich and varied jubilee decorations.

The work of preparing for the celebration was divided; each part was given to a separate committee which worked faithfully to make it a success. The committees and their members were as follows:

Finance—Jere Gordon, Sr., chairman; Thomas Grant, John P. Coffey, P. O'Conor, J. B. J. DuFour.

Invitation and program—F. Chas. Donohue, chairman; John E. Harrington, Jere Gordon, Jr., C. A. McNamara, John Goff.

Music—John L. Carroll, chairman; John P. Lawless, Frank Rogers, John Coyle, John Rau.

Reception—P. E. Cox, chairman; John Tracy, M. Scanlan, P. Reedy, Thomas Carroll, John Sullivan, B. Coyle, Edward Lawless, Owen Brady, James Moore, Robert Casey.

Decorations and fire works—Jere Gordon, Sr., chairman; James J. O'Rourke, A. Lagron, T. D. Osborne, P. Wall, W. R. Barron, Henry Murphy, T. M. Darrah.

Transportation—E. Scanlan, chairman; M. G. Flanagan, T. M. Darrah.

New Dublin—M. McGurk, Gus. Medike, Ed. Manlove, Owen Carmody, Ed. Ledwith, Maurice Hughes.

Irish Grove—A. Mullarkey, James Spellman, D. Mullarkey, Andrew Flynn.

The ladies who labored so well and served so elegantly were:

Dining room—Mesdames James Manion, Jere Reardon, George Hornberger, Louis McGovern, Jennie Markey, Owen Brady, Mrs. M. Madigan, John Sullivan, A. Clermont, P. Ryan; Misses Mary McGovern, Nora Hogan.

Lunch counter—Mesdames John Rau, John Harrington, J. E. Moore, John Burns, John Leary, Jas. McCabe, Misses Maggie Brennan, Maude Gleason, Kate Shay, Maggie Nolan, Kate O'Mara, Mary Wilson, Rose Carey, Maggie Carey, Mabel Moore, Kate Dinley, Alice Goff, Nellie Sweeney, Mary Riley, Anna Nolan, Julia Barron, Lizzie Darrah, Naomi Lagron, Mary Wheeler, Nellie Killion, Lillian Egan, Annie Summers, Mamie Vail, Nellie Burns, Blanche Knipschild, Agnes Dolan, Lillie Dolan, Clara Barron, Kate O'Brien.

Lemonade, etc—Misses Rebecca Vail, Kate Grant, Lizzie Cavanaugh and Sadie Burns.

Badges—Misses Mamie Darrah, Nellie Fagan, Statia Campbell, Nonie Reardon and Rose Gleason.

Church decorations—Miss Mary Darrah, Mesdames J. P. Younger, John Burns, Fanny Cox, P. J. Ryan, J. B. J. Du Four and M. L. Parker.

Reception—Mesdames Fred Kuehner, Robert Casey and John Tracy.

Soliciting out of town—Mesdames John Rau, Jennie Grant, John Rodemeier, F. Fee, A. Clermont, M. Kelley, J. E. Moore; Misses Lucy Barron, Clara Barron and Mary McGovern. In the city—Mesdames Robert Casey, James Manion.

Too much praise cannot be given to the members of the various committees for the efficient manner in which they carried out their plans.

The most important of the jubilee ceremonies was of course the consecration of the church, which took place at seven o'clock on Sunday morning and required nearly three hours' time. The Archbishop of Chicago, Most Rev. P. A. Feehan, officiated, assisted by three bishops and a great number of priests. This ceremony has been of such rare occurrence in the history of the Catholic Church in the west, that in Illinois it has been celebrated but once previous to the occasion under consideration.

The chief requisite that a church may be consecrated, is that it shall be entirely free from debt. The next is that it shall be so located that there is no probability of its ever having to be abandoned and used for some other purpose than the public worship of God. By the ceremonies to which we refer, not only was the church devoted most solemnly to the divine service, but the three altars of marble and onyx were also solemnly consecrated and richly privileged.

On Sunday morning, a succession of low masses were offered, from five o'clock until seven, and at half past ten, a solemn pontifical high mass was sung. The account given in the local papers was interesting and exact; the Democrat gave the following description:

"The first services, in the series prepared for and arranged so carefully by the Rev. Fr. Horan, to be presented at St. Mary's, and which were of great significance to the people of the parish, were successfully and happily carried out, in spite of many misgivings, on the part of those interested, because of the down-pour of rain Saturday night, which threatened to spoil all the preparations and even to cause a postponement of the services. Beyond causing the pastor, and his distinguished guests who were to help him in the celebration, some trepidation, and injuring the appearance of the triumphal arch to some extent, the heavy rainfall did no harm, and ceased in time to allow the performance of the sacred rites of consecration, without interfering with that part of them which occurred outside the church."

"The day which had such an unpleasant beginning became later almost perfect; the skies cleared, the sun quickly dried the streets and by the time the people began to arrive for the pontifical mass, at 10:30 o'clock, the weather had become all that could be desired. On account of the threatening appearance of the morning, there were fewer people came on the excursions from Madison and Rockford, and along the line between the two places, than had been expected, still the number the two special trains brought was considerable, the Rockford delegation bringing a band, which headed the procession as it marched to the church, reaching it just in time for the public services. There were besides, many visitors from the country, who drove in for the day and a great number of families in the parish had guests from a distance who came to attend the jubilee. The visitors were agreeably entertained during the time of their stay by personal friends and members of the reception committee."

"The day's program began at 5 o'clock in the morning, and lasted, with but short intervals, until after vespers in the evening. The first of the services were masses in the chapels of convent and

THE CROWNING OF THE MAY QUEEN AT ST. MARY'S.

church, which were continued until the beginning of the consecration ceremonies at 6:30 o'clock. Though it was barely daylight when the ceremonies commenced, there was a crowd in front of the church to witness the unusual rites, the proceedings being watched with interest. The exterior part of the service occupied half an hour, Archbishop Feehan and those assisting him entering the church at seven o'clock, no one else being admitted, and the service was not concluded until ten. Those taking part in the consecration were the Most Reverend Archbishop Feehan, consecrator; the Reverend Fathers F. S. Henneberry, of Chicago, deacon; B. P. Murray, of Chicago, sub-deacon; E. A. Kelley, of Chicago, M. Foley, of Dixon, and L. X. Du Four, of Mary's, chanters; F. J. Barry, of the Cathedral, Chicago, master of ceremonies, assisted by St. Mary's altar boys."

"After singing the litany of the saints, the archbishop blessed the Gregorian water, which derives its name from Pope St. Gregory the Great, who first ordered this manner of blessing. With the water are mingled salt, ashes and wine, all previously blessed. The water symbolizes: First, the effects of the sacrament of the altar—water, purity of heart; salt, wisdom; ashes, penance, and wine, spiritual joy. Second, Jesus Christ Himself, who is symbolized by the altar; the wine His divine, the water, His human nature, the ashes, His death, the salt His incorruptibility and resurrection."

"The archbishop made the sign of the cross with the blessed water on the altar table, in the center and at the four corners, walked seven times around the altar, sprinkling it with the same water. He mixed cement with holy water and with it sealed the relics in a sepulchre made in the altar stone. Then the archbishop anointed the altar in the center and at both ends with oil and chrism, meanwhile making five signs of the cross over it and incensing it. Out of the blessed incense he made, on the altar, five crosses, each one consisting of five grains of incense, and then covered them with wax. All these crosses were then kindled and allowed to burn away. The incensing, the anointing, and the burning of the crosses have the following meaning: Incense symbolizes favor before God; the holy oil, strength; the chrism, holiness; the burning candles, purifying power; the pouring out together of the holy oil and the chrism, the fullness of every blessing in the sacrifice of Jesus Christ, which, in renewal of the cross, is to be solemnized on this altar."

"Once again, amid prayer, the altar is anointed. Finally the altar cloths are blessed. On these the holy sacrifice was immediately offered up."

"The ceremonies of the consecration of a church consist of the following: On the preceding day, a fast is observed in the parish, and certain prayers are said. In front of the church, the clergy recited the penitential psalms and litany of the

ARCHBISHOP HENNESSEY, OF DUBUQUE.

saints. The archbishop blessed salt and water, with which he sprinkled the outer walls, passing in procession around them three times. At each return, he knocked at the door and asked that it be opened; at the third time, he made on it the sign of the cross, and then it was opened, to show forth that the cross triumphs over all opposition and closes to us the gates of hell."

"The interior is consecrated in the following manner: Uttering the greeting, "Peace be to this house," the archbishop entered and knelt down and invoked the Holy Spirit. While the litany of the saints and the benedictus, Zachary's Canticle of praise were sung, the bishop strewed the floor with ashes, and in them, with his crosier, he wrote the Greek and Latin alphabet. He anointed with chrism, the twelve crosses placed on the walls, called the apostolic crosses, with a lighted taper attached to each. The Greek and Latin alphabets inscribed in the ashes signify that the church is consecrated on the foundation of one Catholic, apostolic faith, which, in the beginning, was proclaimed chiefly in the Greek and Latin languages.' The anointing of the walls at the twelve apostolic crosses, signify that in the edifice the faith will be taught and preached as preached by the twelve apostles."

DESCRIPTION OF THE ALTARS.

"The altars are pure gothic in style. G. S. Mansfield, of this city, was the designer, and the work was done by Schrader & Conraddi, a St. Louis firm. The materials from which they are made are Serravegg or statuary and Blanco marbles, Fredura onyx, agate, Mexican onyx and jasper. The base of the main altar is twelve feet square; the mensa table eight feet long. The altar stands twenty-three feet high from the base and at its widest is sixteen feet. The reredos is of marble, with panels and columns of onyx and the panels are ornamented with jasper. At each side, supporting the tabernacle, are three gold columns which cost $300. On either side of the altar, as it rises above the mensa table, is a Gothic tower, occupied by a representation of a golden winged angel. The side altars are constructed like the main. On altar of the Blessed Virgin is inscribed on a silver plate, "Donated by John Tracy and Family"; on St. Joseph's, "Donated by Joseph Barron and His Sister Lucy." The inscription on the main altar reads, "Donated by the Young Ladies' and Married Ladies' Sodalities."

"The ceremony of consecration having been concluded, the doors were opened and those holding tickets were allowed to pass in. The scene within was indeed beautiful, and words fail to give a true description of the charming decorations. There were draperies of yellow and white looped from the ceiling of the church to the walls on either side, and numerous gold wreaths and loop-

BISHOP BURKE, OF ST. JOSEPH, MO.

ings of the predominant colors on the walls. These loopings were entwined in garlands, and yellow and white flowers were in profusion. Those who were privileged to enter sat in silent contemplation, feasting the eye on the beautiful surroundings until time for the service to begin. The latter was postponed about an hour awaiting the arrival from Rockford of the Catholic Union and the Ancient Order of Hibernians, who came 400 strong as organized bodies, and at 9:30, a half hour later, a delegation of 250 arrived from Madison. The former were accompanied by a band, which discoursed music all the way to the church from the depot. Immediately after the consecration, Archbishop Feehan said low mass at one of the newly consecrated altars."

"Shortly after 10 o'clock, the doors of the church were opened and the people who attended the solemn pontifical mass at 9:30 o'clock began pouring in. Admission was by tickets, with which all the pew holders were provided, and the capacity of the church was increased by crowding chairs as closely together as possible in the aisles. There were many Protestants in the congregation, to whom the services were more impressive on account of their novelty. The limits of the seating capacity were reached fifteen minutes before the orchestra sounded the first note of "Kyrie Eleison," or before the candles on the altar had been lighted. The mass was celebrated by the Rt. Rev. M. Burke, D. D., Bishop of St. Joseph, Mo., assisted by the Very Rev. Father A. O. Walker, O. S. D., of Sinsinawa Mound, archpriest; Rev. Father E. A. Kelley, of Chicago, deacon of the mass; Very Rev. Father Philip O'Connor, of Carroll City, Ia., sub-deacon; Rev. Fathers F. S. Heneberry and B. P. Murray, of Chicago, deacon and sub-deacon of honor; Rev. Father F. J. Barry, master of ceremonies. Archbishop Feehan assisted, with Rev. Fathers Foley and Du Four as chaplains."

"The choir, assisted by Gibler's orchestra, caused the church to resound with such melody as was never heard there before. Generali's grand military mass was rendered; the music was arranged by J. J. Carroll and consisted of the following program:

Kyrie, Andante .... Full chorus
Christe, Andante ..... Mrs. Thro, Miss Tracy, J. P. Lawless, Frank Rogers
Gloria, Allegro. .... Full chorus
Gratias, Moderato..... .. .. John P. Lawless, Ed. Lawless
Domini, Fili, Moderato....................... Misses Carey and Reardon
Domini Deus, Moderato.. Full chorus
Qui Tollis, Larghetto...... .... Mrs. Thro, J. P. Lawless, J. Rau

Qui Sedes, Allegro Moderato.....................Tutti bassos and chorus
Quoniam, Allegretto ....Miss Cunningham
Dei Patris, Allegro Moderato........ ....Finale, full chorus
Credo, Allegretto...................................Unison, full chorus
Genitum, Moderato........:...............................Miss Tracy
Descendit, Moderato.......................................Full chorus

GOLDEN JUBILEE ORCHESTRA AND CHOIR.

Et Incarnatus, Lento...... .... Full chorus
Crucifixus, Lento... ....John and Ed. Lawlers
Et Resurrexit, Allegro......................................Full chorus
Et Iterum, Moderato................... ....Mrs. Thro
Et Inspiritum, Moderato....................................J. P. Lawless
Qui Com Patre, Moderato..................J. P. Lawless, Frank Rogers
Et Unam Sanctam, Moderato.................Misses Carey and Reardon
Et Expecto, Moderato...

"The sermon was delivered by the Rev. Father D. J. Riordan, of St. Elizabeth's church, Chicago, an eloquent and brilliant speaker, his address being closely and logically reasoned, and though extemporized, was perfect in point of rhetoric, his phrases fell gracefully and he spoke with the force of inspiration. Father Riordan arose from a sick bed to attend the jubilee services and at times his voice trembled from weakness, but was not less clear, distinct or musical."

SERMON OF REV. FATHER RIORDAN, SUNDAY, SEPTEMBER 13, 1896.

"The people rejoiced when they promised their gifts willingly, because they offered them to the Lord with all their hearts."

I have chosen this text, my dearly beloved brethren, not indeed with any reference to the subject proper of my remarks to-day, but as expressing, no doubt, the feelings experienced by this congregation of St. Mary's, when some years back, at the invitation of their zealous and devoted pastor, they came together to devise some means of building up a new church to the honor and glory of the eternal God.

It is not well, perhaps, on any occasion to indulge in words of extravagant praise or flattery, yet I fail to see a parallel anywhere in the diocese to the work accomplished here, within the past few years. Whether it be due to your pastor or to yourselves, or to the spirit enkindled and fostered by the devoted, religious Sisters who have charge of your schools, I cannot say, but I think I can say, without giving offense to any one, that it is due to all three combined. To the energy and zeal of your pastor, the generosity of the people, and to the piety and devotedness of the Sisters who have charge of the little ones of this flock. I offer to you, therefore, in my own name, and in the name of the clergy, my heartiest congratulations.

This whole morning, my dearly beloved brethren, was spent in rededicating and in consecrating your church to God. Whatever may have been said of it in the past, from now on, for many years to come, it will be a building dedicated wholly to the service of the Almighty, in which to praise His name. I congratulate you, above all, upon the fact that you can now truly say to

God, that it is His Church. You have paid for it, no man owns it, and it is God's, God's from now on, forever. Accept, therefore, my congratulations, and I trust the people of this parish will always continue to manifest the same spirit of zeal in behalf of their religion; that theirs will not be a religion of faith or belief merely, but that it will be a religion of charity and good works.

This church has been built—what is the object of it—why have the people spent so generously of their means in order to erect a building to the service and worship of God? Is it not, my brethren, because they believe in the truth of their religion—is it not because they are fully convinced that their church is the true church, founded by the Lord and Saviour, Jesus Christ, himself? It would be well for us, during the few remarks I am about to make, to dwell principally upon the reasonableness of the claim of the Catholic church to the acceptance of the faithful Christian. There is perhaps no charge more frequently made, than that the Catholic religion is wholly out of joint with the demands of right reason. It is asserted that no Catholic can accept the teachings of his church without doing violence to the demands and requirements of sound sense. It seems rather strange to us, my brethren, who are members of the fold, that such a charge as this can be made; in fact, we Catholics find it very difficult to acquit thoughtful and religiously disposed people of all blame in refusing to examine, personally, into the astounding claims of a church that has been connected with almost every important event of the past 1900 years—every event that was fraught with weal or woe in the early history of the world.

Let us dwell on these facts briefly this morning, my brethren; briefly I say, because this is due you, on account of the lengthy services of the day, and due perhaps also, in a measure, to myself. Let us dwell briefly, then, upon this subject of the reasonableness of the Catholic faith. Let me endeavor, first of all, to give you some idea of the Church. Starting out with a belief in God, and looking out into the world, we see a condition of things that fills us with distress. Cardinal Newman describes it as full of lamentations, misery and woe, and the apostle, in a few words, describes the condition of the human race, as it passes before us, as being without hope and without God in the world.

Man, my brethren, did not come from the hands of God in the condition in which we find him, and it is not unreasonable to suppose that some great calamity came upon the human race at an early day. Shall we continue by our own unaided efforts to try to remedy this calamity, or shall we seek assistance somewhere else? To say nothing of the impotency of human efforts to right a wrong, such as we suppose must have been committed against the omnipotent God, by the first sin, it is absolutely foolish to expect that man, without the assistance of some superior being, could have come to the relief of the human race. In the first place, the reason of man, unaided by the grace of God, in an environment created by human passions, tends to unbelief, that is to say, the mind of man left to itself, in the condition in which it was created, and subjected to the cravings and demands of the low animal appetites and the sensual passions of human nature, the mind of man, under such circumstances, tends to the elimination of goodness and truth. This appears to be certain when we study the history of the past. What was the outcome of the old pagan religion, but the rejection of all true ideas of God?

Many of our unassisted, advanced thinkers of to-day, have adopted a new idea of religion, and they are preaching the unknowable and humanitarianism as the outcome of their best individual efforts.

It is not unreasonable, therefore, to suppose that the Almighty God himself came to the rescue of the human race; there is a fitness in this, all the greater when we come to consider the great goodness of God. He first made man in His own image and likeness, and what was more, was determined that the great work of the Creator of the world and of man should not come to naught. This brings us, therefore, to the incarnation of the Son of God. Man being unable to remedy the great defects and overcome the calamity and consequences of the first great disaster, God comes to his rescue. The Eternal Son of God himself became man. Why did Christ become man? Only a Catholic, it seems to me, can answer that question satisfactorily. Let us bear in mind, my brethren, that our divine Lord is the Saviour of all mankind, of you and me, as well as of those who shall come after us, and we can say, with the same truth as the apostles of old, " My Lord and my God."

Christ is the one Saviour of the world, and there is one God, and Lord, so one faith and one baptism.

REV. D. J. RIORDAN,
Pastor of St. Elizabeth's Church, Chicago, Ill.

Now, our Lord lived but a short time on this earth, then He was crucified and He died. How was His work to be perpetuated? He established a church—a church that was to endure throughout all the ages of the world and to continue the work which He came to accomplish. The Church is the witness, and Jesus Christ is the teacher of the truths which He made known to His apostles. This is the means by which the sanctifying grace of Christ is brought home to the individual, and by which each and every one of us can hope to save our souls. That is the nature and the object of the Church. How does it accomplish its purpose? Founded by Christ, and by Him invested with His own authority, the Church is not a creation of men, or any number of men; it is not the work of the Pope, the Bishops or the Priests, but the work of Christ. In the sense in which you say God made the earth, and that He spread the sky over our heads, in that same sense do we say that Christ, with His own divine authority, without respect to the wishes of man, without counseling with him, founded the Church, which was to take His place, and be to all people, to the end of the world, what He himself was to the people of His own day; what He would have been to the people of this day, and to the people to come, had He continued to live on in the world. Is there any other religious denomination that claims this divine authority? Well, in theory there is, but hardly in practice, and the great fundamental truth after all, is the divine establishment of the Christian Church, with the authority of the divine Founder, to preach and teach in His name. The Church does not argue with the people, the apostles did not argue, they announced the truths of their God, they commanded people to hear them, they bore in mind the words of the Divine Master himself, who said, "He that heareth you heareth Me, and he that despiseth you, despiseth Me."

Sometimes I hear people say, "Well, there is not so much difference between your church and ours. We have vestments, we have lights and acolytes, yes, we have even the confessional, with few, I fear, of the awful secrets." Now, why should similarity, or dissimilarity in these things constitute a resemblance or dissemblance between the various churches? The great difference between the Church, and all other churches is this—that the Church stands instead of Christ, that she preaches in God's name, that she comes with authority from the eternal Son of God, the Founder of the Christian religion.

She does not ask, and does not permit people to inquire into her teachings; of her own authority, she announces the truths taught by the Divine Saviour of the world. The controversy, in the past 300 years has been, for the most part, upon side issues;

little, or comparatively little, has been said upon this vital fundamental thought, namely—the authority of the Church. Now, my brethren, is there anything unreasonable in the claim of the Church to the authority of Christ, since Christ founded

BISHOP JANSEN.

it to be a witness to Him, and a teacher of His truths throughout all ages? We are not without authority, of course, in the treatment of this subject, but we now confine ourselves wholly to what may appear reasonable to the mind, especially, if debating with those who are not in accord with us in religious matters. If we fell back upon the inspired word of God, and then found that this book, which gives the history of the life of Jesus Christ, the Founder of the Church, was silent upon this most salient point, it would be most disappointing to us. But, as we read this inspired book, we see many pages, where we find acceptable reference to this very point, and we are told, again and again, by the apostles, that they were sent out into the world to teach, in the name of Christ, that they have His own authority, and that of the Eternal Father who sent Him. So, also, He sent them to teach the universal world, and to proclaim to all mankind the great tidings of the Gospel. Here, therefore, according to this scriptural teaching, here is a picture of the Church. A body of men, appointed by public ceremony, invested with divine authority, inculcating the truths of religion, not in their own name, not in the name of advanced thinkers and scientists, but in the name of the Founder of Christianity, and declaring that all men must believe them, under pain of an anathema. "He that heareth you, said the Lord, heareth Me, and he that despiseth you, despiseth Me."

I merely claim, my brethren, that it is not unreasonable to suppose that Christ founded the Church ; it is not unreasonable to suppose that the Church is invested with the authority of its divine Founder.

It is said of us: "Catholics will believe anything"; "not only do members of the Church claim authority to preach in the name of God, but they claim infallibility for the Church"; they say " 'the Church cannot err in matters of religion;' how can a fallible man become infallible, how can a man, subject to all the weaknesses of human nature, one who, like all others, has felt the heavy hand of the first curse laid upon our first parents—how can such a man expect to be exempt from error?"

If you and I are obliged to believe in a Church, why that Church must be protected in some way, by Almighty God, from leading you and me astray. Is it impossible for God to confer on man the gift of infallibility? I can imagine a thousand ways in which God is able to protect a human mind from error; He

BISHOP S. G. MESSMER.

can reveal himself to each and every one of us, so we will be absolutely sure of the teachings of our minds. He can bring about such a result by external means. Did not God make the human mind—can He not guide it, and direct it, and lead it wherever He will? The discussion is foolish from every point of view. How can people find fault with the bestowal of such a gift? We have to admit the inspiration of the Scriptures. Who wrote the Bible—did God? Did God take a pen in His own hands and write the words which I have read for you to-day? The authors and writers were men, God's chosen disciples, and yet you and I, and all of us, accept it as the written word of God. Now, if God could protect them, by means of special inspiration, from falling into any error while they were writing the sacred pages of the Gospel, why can He not protect one or more men, and guard them, against all error, in matters appertaining to the most important of all, the salvation of their souls? In fact, what would be the good of establishing a church, and authorizing that church to preach the Gospel, unless the seal and stamp of the Divinity was put upon the work itself? Those He had appointed not only claimed authority to preach in His name, but were assisted by some special aid of the Holy Ghost to enable them, at all times, to declare the truth, the whole truth and nothing more.

I must not, my dearly beloved brethren, detain you too long this morning. The subject is certainly an inviting one and a most attractive one, and I might, did time permit, enlarge upon many of the most disputed points of the Catholic doctrine, in order to show you how reasonable, from the information imparted by the Holy Scriptures, are these various teachings of the Catholic Church. As to the claims of the Catholic Church, they may be illustrated by the following example:

Suppose we were about to take a long journey; at first our way led by a broad avenue through an open country, but soon we come to the foot-hills in the mountain range, where we find different roads, and then, as we are about to enter, certain guides present themselves. One claims to know the way—he is absolutely certain he can lead us to our destination. The others claim only a probability, they are not sure they are right, they think themselves sufficiently familiar with the way not to lead us astray, but are not quite certain. I ask you which one of these guides would you choose, did you feel bound to reach the objective point? Why, surely you would choose the guide who claims to know the way. He may be mistaken, he may not be able to lead you aright, but you cannot act according to the claims of sound sense and prudence if you select the guide who tells you he is not sure he is right. If you select him, you act unreasonably, at the start; you will dispute with him every step, and at every turning point in the way you will stop him. What is this but a picture of the blind leading the blind, and both falling into the pit? If you select the guide who claims to know the way, once you have placed yourself under his guidance, you will follow him quietly, never interfering, feeling assured that he will lead you aright. Is not this, then, the relative position of the Catholic Church with all other churches? The Church claims to know the way.

"I am the Church of the living God." She says: "I am the Church founded by the Lord and Saviour Jesus Christ. I was not born yesterday, or the last century—I have a history that goes back through all ages; if you will follow me, I will lead you in the road that will take you to eternal life."

Are we not apt, brethren to believe this honest, direct and forcible presentation of the claims of the Catholic Church, even though it be made by ourselves?

Strangers, who are not in our communion, have sometimes drawn very forcible and vivid pictures of the Church.

I will ask your permission to read to you what the distinguished author, Mallock, has written on the subject now being treated. (Here the Rt. Rev. speaker read an extract, of which we have no copy.)

Here is a picture of the Church drawn by a stranger; he draws it well, but it does not satisfy the Catholic; it does not satisfy the man who has been born in the Church, who looks into the eyes of his living mother, with a heart full of tenderness and keen sense of the weighty debt he owes her. The faith of the Catholic is something akin to that gift which nature bestows upon the childish heart, a faith abounding in love.

The true character of the Church cannot be perfectly described; it must be felt in the heart. The Church, my brethren, is the road to our Lord and Saviour Jesus Christ, and, through Him, to heaven. In her, the Christian hears the voice of the Lord himself.

In the heavenly picture of the world to come, he feels a sense of security, and is overjoyed by a participation in the feeling experienced by the apostle on Mount Thabor when he exclaimed, "Lord, it is good for us to be here." In life's experiences, the Catholic always feels secure; he knows the Church will lead him aright. Knowledge and power are the two great requisites for the success of every enterprise. The Church possesses them in all their fullness. She is the truth—she has the strength of God to lead her aright.

Therefore, my brethren, when we kneel down in this Church to worship Almighty God, first professing our faith in God, the Father, the Son and the Holy Ghost, we will ever exclaim in all the fullness and love of our heart, "I believe in the Holy Catholic Church."

THE JUBILEE CHOIR.

The musical part of the service was of unusual merit, and would have rendered the occasion memorable, even if there had been no other attractions. The best singers of both congregations, St. Joseph's and St. Mary's, joined under the significant title, "The Jubilee Choir," and, by diligent practice, fitted themselves to produce magnificent results. On the great days that were successively celebrated, they were assisted by Gibler's orchestra. At the mass that followed the consecration of the church, Generali's grand military mass in G was sung in parts as follows:

Kyrie..Full Chorus
Christi..Quartette
    Soprano, Mrs. Leo Thro; alto, Miss Jennie Tracy; tenor, J. P. Lawless;
        bass, Frank Rogers.

Gloria..Full Chorus
Gratia... Duet
        Tenor, J. P. Lawless; baritone, Ed. Lawless.
Domine Fili...Duet
        Soprano, Miss Maggie Carey; alto, Miss Nonie Reardon.
Domine Deus..Full Chorus
Qui Tollis... ....Trio
        Soprano, Mrs. Leo Thro; tenor, J. P. Lawless; bass, John Rau.
Qui Sedes...Basses and Chorus
Quonian..Solo
        Miss Cunningham.
Dei Patris...Full Chorus
Credo..Full Chorus
Genitum... .Mezzo Soprano Solo
        Miss Jennie Tracy.
Descendit..Full Chorus
Et Incarnatus Est..Full Chorus
Crucifixus ....Duet
        Tenor, J. P. Lawless; baritone, Ed. Lawless.
Et Resurrexit...Full Chorus
Et Interum..Soprano Solo
        Mrs. Leo Thro.
Et In Spiritum...Tenor Solo
        J. P. Lawless.
Qui Cum Patre. ....Duet
        Tenor, J. P. Lawless; bass, Frank Rogers.
Et Unam Sanctam...Duet
        Soprano, Miss Maggie Carey; alto, Miss Nonie Reardon.
Et Expecto..Full Chorus
Finale ...:... Full Chorus
Offertorium ....O Cor Amoris Victima
        Full chorus with soprano solo obligato by Mrs. Leo Thro.
Sanctus..Full Chorus
Pleni ....Full Chorus
Benedictus...Alto Solo
        Miss Jennie Tracy with cello obligato by Oscar Wagner.
Hosanna...Full Chorus
Agnus Dei ....''...Full Chorus
        With tenor solo by J. P. Lawless; soprano solo by Mrs. Leo Thro.
Dona Nobis, Finale..Full Chorus

    The members of the Jubilee Choir were: Director, John L. Carroll; organist, Miss Mary E. Brennan; orchestra director, W.

H. Gibler; soloists: W. H. Gibler, violin; Mrs. Leo Thro and Miss Maggie Carey, sopranos; Miss Jennie P. Tracy, mezzo soprano; Miss Nonie Reardon, contralto; Miss Cunningham, alto; John P. Lawless, tenor; Edward Lawless, baritone; John Rau and Frank Rogers, bassos. Chorus: Sopranos, Mrs. M. Ellsworth, Misses Susie Ellis, Anna Summers, Gertrude Loos, Josie Wilson, Blanche Knipschild, Loretta Knipschild, Mamie Vail, Agnes Dolan; altos, Misses Theresa Loos, Josie Nohe, Anna Darrah, Theresa Miller, Helen Miller; tenors, Herman Straub, Frank Burns, John Loos; bassos, John Coyle, Leo Thro, Clem Gordon and Ed. Dubs.

ARCHBISHOP FEEHAN'S ADDRESS.

Archbishop Feehan also spoke briefly at the morning service, congratulating the congregation upon having that day given to God so magnificent a temple, and praising highly the Pastor, the Sisters of the school and the members of the congregation for their work. "This day," he said, "will be long known as one of the greatest in the history of the parish. Fifty years to the church, or to history, are but a span, but in the lives of individuals, or congregations, they are a great deal. The celebration of this Golden Jubilee is an occasion of much pleasure. Sincere is the joy afforded by the knowledge that the Catholics of this diocese have been able to make such an offering to God as this church. The consecration gives it to Him forever; it can never be given for any other use, or destroyed, except by some great calamity.

"How different is the congregation of to-day from the one that first met fifty years ago! The few who assembled for the first mass have grown and multiplied to a great congregation, like a tiny seed that has grown to a great tree. Those pioneers who first came here, and among whom the faith was so firmly established, deserve all honor from us. They have nearly all gone to their rest, and we can hardly realize the trials and struggles they have endured. They brought with them the one priceless pearl, their religious faith; they were loyal to it, in all their hardships, and bequeathed their loyalty to their children and their children's children, who are here to-day to celebrate this Golden Jubilee. We must not forget the priests who labored in the building up of this church, who came with the pioneers, and, suffering what they did, earned a share in the result. There was another element of success, the daughters of Ireland, who, as religious teachers, and as faithful mothers of families, followed the teachings of priests and missionaries and cared for the young. All worked together to build up the Church all through this new land. Fifty years is not long, but see the result! Who could have foretold, when they were planting the seed, that the harvest would be so splendid? The congregation of this church may well rejoice.

"There is another thought: we ask ourselves, 'What kind of people will come after us? Will they be loyal and cling to the high principles of the pioneers; will they be men of character, true to their religion and cherishing their faith?' To-day finds the answer. The praise given to-day is well deserved. It is a source of great gratification to see the success of the Church and the school. Upon the latter rests the future of the Church; in the training of the young, the planting of good seeds and the awakening of a lively faith in the minds of the children, lies the secret of large, zealous congregations for the future."

The mass was not ended until after one o'clock, but nothing further took place at St. Mary's until evening, when there was a pontifical-vesper service, at which Bishop Janssen presided, and all the visiting clergymen assisted. A short sermon was delivered by Bishop Burke, who spoke of the sacredness of the church, since it had been anointed, with holy oil, and consecrated to the service of God.

The vespers, the sermon and the benediction of the Blessed Sacrament, in the glory of lights and song, constituted one of the most impressive services held during the week. The sanctuary was filled with richly vested clergymen of various ranks; the altar boys, in their pretty robes, were present, in full force, and sang the vespers, alternately with the grand choir, in a style never before equaled by them. Finally, so inspiring was the scene and the music, all the clergymen joined in chanting the psalms and hymns, making a magnificent chorus of supplication and adoration, that seemed to the listeners a foretaste of heavenly harmony and celestial song.

The gleaming tapers and the flashing gas lights, with the steady radiance of electricity, brought out all the beauties of the altars and their surroundings, so that sight, as well as hearing, was enthralled.

Between the vesper and the benediction services, Bishop Burke, of St. Joseph, Mo., delivered his eloquent discourse, referred to above. In beautiful language, he told the story of the cross, what Christ had done for mankind, and urged all to follow in His footsteps. He also spoke words of praise in regard to the beautiful house of worship which the members of St. Mary's congregation had erected. He said it was a lasting monument to their devotion and their zeal for the cause of Christ, and admonished the members ever to remember that it was a sacred place, which they should enter with only pure thoughts in their hearts. He complimented Rev. Father Horan, on the great work he has accomplished, since coming to Freeport, and said that the reverend gentleman could not have accomplished this, were it not for the fact that he possessed the confidence and love of his people, in a marked degree. Bishop Burke is a dignified and polished gentleman who makes a fine appearance in the pulpit. He is noted for his piety and scholarly attainments. There was a congregation present that overflowed the church, and great numbers of people sought admission who could not find a place to either sit or stand.

The Golden Jubilee Day.

With all the pomp and splendor of the highest functions of the Roman Catholic Church, the Golden Jubilee of the establishment of the Catholic religion in this county was celebrated on October 14th. The first few of the fifty years that have intervened were filled with struggles, cares and hardships, with disappointments and heavy trials; the last few have been marked by thrift and ultimate success, but, at all times, there have been unremitting toil and dogged perseverence. This day's celebration is the climax of the pious events of the past half century, and the realization of the most sanguine hopes of the early priests and their pioneer congregations. Their zeal and loyal perseverence prepared the way for this day, and made its celebration possible. Through their efforts, in the almost barren days of the county's early history, was sown a great part of the seed that has grown into the rich harvest of to-day.

The large, respectable and attentive congregations that assembled in St. Mary's each day, during the great celebration, the church itself, with its chaste and beautiful altars, the soft, religious light, beaming through rare stained windows, the roll of the organ, the swell of the orchestra and the volume of fifty voices in choir, the number and high rank of the ecclesiastics, in rich and gorgeous vestments, celebrating the mass,—all this contrasted, strongly and strangely, with the first congregation of twenty devout souls, assembled in a log cabin, or in the simple home of the pioneer priest and his sister. No organ, no choir rejoiced their ears; neither acolyte nor altar boy served the priest standing at the improvised altar, and no rich vestments, or costly altar furniture, added impressiveness to the sacred ceremonies. Faith, simple, fervent and unquestioning; piety, warm and enduring; charity, prompt and generous—these were the sole riches of the pioneer, and who shall say whether he were not a millionaire, compared with Catholic Christians of our day? The contrast in externals was great, indeed; perhaps it was surpassed, in an opposite sense, by the interior differences.

In the early times, there was little of the magnificent show of symbolism, little display of the power and grandeur of the Roman Catholic Church, as seen in these festival ceremonies. There existed then none of the conditions so essential to the pomp and dignity of the pontifical mass, that was offered each morning during the three days' celebration. These pioneers brought with them into the wilderness, they were to conquer and make fruitful, the early faith, which took root and flourished, until it has come to have as much force and influence, as in olden countries, where much longer established.

The services, on Sunday, Oct. 13, were only indirectly connected with the jubilee celebration; they were preparatory, and the consecration of the church previous to the celebration of the Jubilee Mass, added to the grace and thankfulness with which the latter was offered, on Monday morning, Oct. 14. The elements were kind on Sunday, the sky clearing, after the night's rain, but Monday morning the rain, that unexpectedly began to come down in sheets before daylight, continued to fall until noon, and, though it did not interfere with any of the church arrangements, it kept a great many people at home, who would otherwise have attended the ceremonies.

The services began with the low masses at 5 o'clock, as on Sunday. At 9:30, Archbishop Feehan confirmed a class of about fifty boys and girls, who remained, after confirmation, to assist at the Jubilee Mass. By 10:15 o'clock the church was comfortably filled.

Bishop Dunne, of Dallas, Texas, was to have sung the pontifical mass for the Golden Jubilee Day, but illness kept him at home, hence Bishop Burke was the celebrant, Archbishop Feehan being present in the sanctuary. The number of priests in attendance was much larger than on Sunday. The Jubilee Sermon was preached by Archbishop Hennessey, of Dubuque. His discourse was a forceful, logical, argumentative one. He is a powerful and graceful speaker. The following is a somewhat imperfect reproduction of his sermon:

SERMON BY ARCHBISHOP HENNESSEY.

Allow me to congratulate you on the fiftieth anniversary of the Roman Catholic Church in Freeport, and on the magnificence of the ceremonies of this festival.

To-day the Catholic Church celebrates the Feast of the Exaltation of the Holy Cross, which commemorates the restoration of the Holy Cross, taken from Jerusalem early in the seventh century by the Saracens and restored later in the century by Heraclius, emperor of Constantinople.

St. Paul tells us we should glory in the Cross of Christ, and the restoration of the Cross to the Church commends it. I deem it my duty to endeavor to show you the relations which you bear to the Cross of Jesus Christ, and your dependence on it, in time and in eternity.

Brethren, we were made for heaven. We were made for happiness. When God made man, He united the body and the soul; the soul was the life of the body; it was the intelligent force, but there was another element, which was the light of the soul; it is the light of the Lord within the soul. These three elements constitute the man of God, and, brethren, without these three elements, no man can enter into the kingdom of heaven. If there is no life in the soul, no soul within a soul, the individual shall never know the happiness for which he is made. The life of the soul shall shield the life of the body, and if it had been preserved, there would have been no death, either of the soul or of the body, in time or in eternity. But the life of the soul was unfortunately lost, and then was broken that special bond by which God united man to himself. Man fell; he fell dead, as to his soul, and under sentence of death, as to his body. he was dead also in all the powers and faculties of both soul and body.

The condition of the first man passed to his descendants, just as children are born into slavery; the condition of the father passing to the children, so the condition of Adam passed to all his descendants, for Adam was the father of the human race; and the human race was in Adam, as the oak is in the acorn, and when he fell, when he broke the bond that united him to God, the whole human race fell with him, dead as to their souls, crippled in all their faculties, and, being subject to the power of evil spirits, became strongly inclined to the commission of evil deeds.

So much, brethren, for the effects of one little sin; it is quite common amongst us to treat it as such, but to the all holy God, who sees sin as it really is, it is infinitely hateful. Evil is of the world, and not of God; it is an uprising against God; an act in defiance of the omnipotence of God; it is using God's gifts against himself.

By sin, we practically deny the sovereignty of God, an attribute which is essential to God. Deprive anything of an essential property, and you thereby destroy it. Deprive a triangle of one of its three angles and the triangle is gone. Deprive a quadrangle, having four equal sides, of one of the right angles, and you have a quadrangle no longer. Deprive God of His sovereignty, and there is no God; then, if it were possible for God to die, sin would have caused His death. When God became man, took upon Himself our mortality, sin struck Him the fatal blow, in His humanity, since it might not attack His divinity.

Read the history of the human race, behold the work of the black passions of the human heart; how man hates man, how man wreaks his vengeance upon man. Wars, famines and other ravages, have come into every land, and the Gospel is everywhere torn into shreds.

Listen to the groans of sinners; listen to their lamentations, which will be unavailing through all eternity. Look, then, at the Son of God; See Him in the Garden of Gethsemane, bleeding in every pore, covered with blood; His heart is breaking and He cries to God, "O Father, if it be possible, let this cup pass from me!" Then He is dragged through the streets of Jerusalem, and, after enduring further indignities, He hangs to the cross, crying out in His pain, "My God, my God, why hast thou forsaken me?"

Again, God did not deal with man as He dealt with the angels, He did not leave man in the fallen state; He decreed that man should be reborn and restored to the dignity for which he was created; and how was this to be done?

MR. AND MRS. R. BARRON.

God might have forgiven the debt, as a creditor forgives the debt his neighbor owes him. God might have accepted partial satisfaction, but He did not do it. In His justice and His wisdom, He saw it was better for man that He demand full satisfaction for the outrage offered Him, and He made that demand of man. The demand was for infinite satisfaction; man could not make it; the whole human race could not make it; how, then, was it to be made? God's Son came to earth; "It is written that I shall do thy will, O God!" So God's eternal Son came down to earth; He united man to God; He became a man with a body like ours; He had a man's nature and being, that He might go to the altar and offer sacrifices and atone for our sins, and He did go, and satisfied the most rigorous demands of justice, and won for us merits of infinite value. He won life for us by His death. He bequeathed His infinite merits to us; they are our legacy; they are our all. I wish you could realize the solemn fact that no man has ever entered heaven, that no man has ever escaped death, except through these merits. It is not enough that He won these for us, that He bequeathed them to us, we must appropriate them, must make use of them. A man may die of thirst, beside a fountain, if he will not stoop down to drink; he may die of hunger, in a banquet hall, if he will not eat. We are debtors, indeed, for rich and freely given treasures, and we have no right to find fault, if we make no use of what the Lord has tendered us gratuitously.

How are these merits communicated to us? This is a most important question, one which you should thoroughly consider. You will say, perhaps, that they will be communicated to us in the manner in which He wills.

He made us as we are; without Him, nothing was made; He made us composed of a soul and body, and such is our nature that spritual things come to us through the bodily senses. Our senses are the avenues of the soul; so there is nothing in the finite human being which has not been received through the senses.

Look at the children in school; how do they learn? One man has knowledge that another has not; he wishes to communicate it; how will he do it? He will put his thoughts and ideas into words, and then he will give utterance to his words; he exercises certain parts of his body, and thus sends forth his words. They are received into the ear, and are presented to the intellect of his hearer, who then accepts them and the knowledge that comes with them. Thus an idea passes through two bodies before it reaches the soul of the person taught. Such is nature of man; in this way does he learn and receive the truth.

God classified the spiritual wants of the human race under seven heads, and then He instituted seven channels through which these needs could be supplied. By one of these seven ceremonies, He gives the soul life, makes a soul within a soul, as it were; by another, He perpetuates men who are to demonstrate these ceremonies and minister them for Christ, as Christ's representatives; by another, the bond of marriage, He perpetuates the Church and her children, that in her and for them, these wonderful works may take place.

Why should any one man profess to know more than another, to have greater powers than another, and why should any man bow down his head before another man, while praying to the Father, Son and Holy Ghost, to cleanse his soul from sin, unless there was a divine reason for it?

Why should he throw himself upon his knees before the son of a neighbor, whom he may have known years before, as a school boy? Why, on bended knees, and with weeping eyes, does he make known to this man the secrets of his life, unless he is convinced that his neighbor's son can do something for him? To conduct these ceremonies, human teaching and human agency is required. Human agency has been employed because the service of God is always a reasonable service. From among His disciples, then, Jesus Christ chose twelve to be teachers, and He placed one of these, St. Peter, at the head of the others, and, with St. Peter at the head, He formed a living body. Just as you do when you form a society; you always elect a president. In order that the effect of their teaching should last to the end of time, they were authorized, even commanded, to teach to the end of time.

Brethren, seventy years from that time, every one of these twelve had passed away. How were their places to be filled? Christ made a corporate body; a corporate body never dies. It is like the city council; you have aldermen and a mayor; when they go out of office, others take their places; the council is continued as a living corporation. Thus was this corporation to continue in the future, and our Lord determined the manner in which the corporation was to continue; how the places of those who had passed away should be filled; He made them teachers, and commanded them to teach the nations; there were to be none left out. They were to teach in the name of Jesus Christ; they were to be free from error; that is to say, in delivering His message, they delivered it just as they received it. He made them infallible. The message He gave to this corporation of twelve was needed by the nations. It was His message, and, as it came from the corporation, was no counterfeit, but the message as it came from the lips of Jesus Christ.

Brethren, if you were sending a message to a friend, and his life depended upon the receipt of it and compliance with its requirements, would you not choose a messenger whom you could trust to deliver it? The lives of those whom Jesus Christ taught depended on receiving His message. Was He not able to send His message so it would surely be delivered? Was He not willing to do it? If He had not delivered it to reliable persons, the message would have been lost, and the whole work and labor of His life would have been lost. But He did not leave His message to chance—He did not leave it to any family. He sent an escort with it to guard it, and that escort was Himself. He had said, "I will send the Holy Ghost, the Spirit of Truth, to abide with you forever," and, having thus guarded His message, He can say to His ministers, "He that hears you, hears Me; your words are my words; you teachings are my teachings; your message is the message I gave you. I give it to you for my people, and to the peril of their souls they must receive it. He that hears and believes shall be saved, but he that hears and believes not shall be damned."

"They dare not refuse my teachings, for if they do, it shall be at the peril of their souls; they shall be damned." Who but a God of Justice could pronounce such a sentence? This corporation was the infallible teacher of the Gospel for all time. St. Paul said of the apostles that they were ministers of Christ, and dispensers of the mysteries of God.

Teaching did not sanctify men; teaching did not make them holy, or fit them for heaven, or put into them that soul within a soul, existing to the honor of God.

When men had received their teaching, what did the apostles do? They baptised them. St. Paul baptised in the name of the Father and of the Son and of the Holy Ghost. "Unless a man be born again of water and of the Holy Ghost, he cannot enter the kingdom of God."

You go through the ceremony of baptism and become new creatures, children of God and of His Church. Baptising in the Holy Ghost, that is what St. Peter and St. John did, and thus did the soul receive life, true life; every life that is, comes from God and every life that comes from God bears life. Every life that comes from God needs sustenance, and the just God provides it. The plant lives, but not without nourishment; the flowers in the field must have nourishment. Man eats three times a day to preserve his bodily life. There is the same need in his spiritual life, hence God furnishes bread for the soul, that is life and that gives life. He said, "And the bread I will give is my flesh, and the wine is my blood, shed for the life of the world, and unless you eat of the flesh of the Son of man and drink His blood, you shall not have life everlasting." Thus He gave His apostles His own flesh and blood, saying, "Do this in commemoration of me; do what you have seen me do; change bread into my body and wine into my blood, and minister to the people, as you have seen me do." They did this and went from house to house, breaking bread and giving the flesh of Jesus Christ and the blood of Jesus Christ to His followers. Thus they fed the soul, that its life might not be lost. Adam had lost it by his sin against God; they were to forgive sins; it was said to them, "Men's sins you shall forgive. You have power of forgiving sins and of refusing to forgive them." This twofold power could not be exercised reasonably, without a knowledge of the sins to be forgiven: without a knowledge of the sinner. This knowledge must come from himself, must come from his own lips, and that communication from his lips is what we call confession, and thus the faithful confess their sins, knowing they will be forgiven. Some one will say, "How can man forgive sins?" That has been said a thousand times, but we must remember these were not ordinary men; they were ministers of Jesus Christ, officers of His mysteries. To forgive sins is to restore life; God alone can do that; God alone lives and is the source of life; He alone can restore life when it is lost.

Sts. Peter and Paul did this by the power of God. They restored the dead to life, and if God employed human agency to restore dead bodies, why may He not do the same to restore dead souls? To raise a dead soul is not more difficult than to raise a dead body. He does this work through His ministers: they likewise anoint the sick with oil and prepare them to meet their God.

And the bond of marriage; it is the very foundation of society. It, too, has the seal of Jesus Christ, and its object is to make one grand family, uniting in the world all who are Christ's, and uniting, likewise, the Church and the State.

The acts, whereby these great powers were conferred on the apostles, were public; they were done before men. This teaching was heard; these ceremonies were seen, and the effects of both will continue until the end of time. That corporation will ever exist to carry on, to the consummation of the world, the work assigned it. That body has never lost its identity; it is the same to-day, as it was when our Lord formed it. It will be the same to the end of time. James or John may be thirty years old, forty years old, or fifty years old, but he does not lose his identity; he remains the same individual. So does this body, whether it is twelve months or five hundred years old.

Brethren, where is that body to-day? It exists and will exist to the end of time. Where is it? It is public and ought to be known. It is not hiding; it is on the hill-tops, and it is very active. The Bishops of the holy Catholic Church are members of this body; they have been in the world for 1800 years; they have been doing all the apostles did in their day. You can trace them back as easily as you can trace the presidents, from Cleveland to Washington; you can trace them back from Leo XIII. to St. Peter. Every link in the chain is complete; not one is wanting. When one head of the body has passed away, another has taken his place; just like the mayor and the council. The Bishops, with the Pope of Rome at their head, have ever claimed infallibility in their teaching, and they are the only body of men who have it, moreover they challenge the world to disprove their claim.

JOHN L. CARROLL,
LEADER.

EDWARD LAWLESS.

MISS M. BRENNAN,
ORGANIST.

JOHN H. RAU.

JOHN P. LAWLESS.

Brethren, look over the history of the world; does it show you any other body or corporation that has existed for 1800 years, teaching and dispensing the mysteries of God, as the Bishops of the Roman Catholic Church do? No, ten thousand times no. As there is but one sun in the heavens to light the earth, there is but one sun of justice, our Redeemer, Jesus Christ, to light the Church; one Lord, one baptism, one Church and one corporation which is to work until the end of time.

Verily, brethren, there are no persons, members of a corporation, among those around you, who are ready to serve you at all times, except the apostles and their successors. They will deliver to you the message Jesus Christ sent you; they will give you the truth of the Holy Ghost, and redeem your soul, through the merits of Jesus Christ. Have you that life of the soul that comes through Jesus Christ, through the ceremonies He has instituted to be administered by His chosen ministers? Now is the time to receive these ministers; to hear these words that give life to the soul. Why not receive them now? They alone can forgive sins, and thus restore the life to the soul, through the merits of Jesus Christ. Will you then allow your souls to remain dead? It is an all important question that I leave you to consider.

To appreciate this discourse, the reader should have heard it delivered in that decisive and convincing manner which characterizes the public utterances of His Grace of Dubuque.

The music given by the Jubilee Choir on Monday, during the ceremonies of confirmation, was as follows:

Veni Creator—

Mezzo Soprano..................................Miss Jennie Tracy
Tenor...J. P. Lawless
Baritone......................................Ed. Lawless
With full chorus.

At the celebration of the Golden Jubilee "Missa pro pace" (mass for peace), by T. Von La Hache, was sung as presented in this programme:

Kyrie...Full Chorus
Gloria..Full Chorus
Et in Terra...................................Full Chorus

MISS M. CAREY.

MRS. LEO THRO.

MISS J. P. TRACY.

MRS. M. ELLSWORTH.

MISS N. REARDON.

Gratias, soprano solo.. .... Mrs. Leo Thro
Qui Tollis... Bassos and Chorus
Quoniam, soprano solo.............................. Miss Maggie Carey
Finale Quoniam... Full Chorus
Credo.. Full Chorus
Visibilium, soprano solo..'........................... Mrs. Leo Thro
Genitum.. Bassos and Chorus
Et incarnatus est, soprano solo .... Mrs. Leo Thro
Crucifixus, soprano solo with full chorus. .... Mrs. Leo Thro
Et Resurrexit, duet with full chorus.................................
................Soprano, Miss Maggie Carey; tenor, J. P. Lawless
Et in Spiritum, bass solo........ .... John Rau
Qui Cum Patre, soprano solo........................... Mrs. Leo Thro
Finale .... Full Chorus
Offertorium, Ave Maria, violin obligato...W. H. Gibler, Miss Jennie Tracy
Sanctus, soprano solo, obligato........................ Mrs. Leo Thro
 With full chorus.
Benedictus, soprano solo obligato..................... Mrs. Leo Thro
 With chorus accompaniment.
Agnus Dei—
Baritone Solo.. Ed. Lawless
Soprano Solo.. Miss Maggie Carey
Tenor Solo.. J. P. Lawless
 With full chorus accompaniment.
Dona Nobis and Finale................................... Full Chorus

While all who were connected with the jubilee services merited the heartiest congratulations for the magnificence and splendor of the ceremonies, high praise is due to those who prepared the music rendered at the Sunday morning service. Generali's military mass was beautifully sung by the Jubilee Choir, assisted by Gibler's Orchestra, and was one of the most important parts of the musical programme. On Monday, La Hache's mass was no less satisfactorily given, and added impressiveness to the solemn ceremonials. The chief credit for the excellence of the music is due to John L. Carroll, who worked indefatigably, for three months, to get the masses ready for satisfactory production. They were all long and difficult, but they were mastered, and both the solos and choruses were sung with precision and good effect, being altogether the most beautifully rendered sacred music ever heard in this city.

The music at St. Joseph's Church was also of a high order, particularly the Millard Mass, by the Jubilee Choir, and St. Pius' Choir.

THE CHILDREN'S RECEPTION.

One of the prettiest events of the jubilee festival was the reception for Archbishop Feehan arranged by the Feehan Reading Circle of St. Mary's High School. Illness prevented the Archbishop from attending, but Bishop Burke was present, and the program was carried out as intended. At its close, the Bishop spoke briefly, praising the work and intentions of the circle.

The program was given in St. Mary's Hall, which was prettily decorated, and there was a large audience present, including nearly all the clergymen who were Father Horan's guests for the day. The entertainment was opened by an address by Clement Gordon, as follows:

"MOST REV. AND DEAR FATHER: It is with the deepest sentiments of affectionate reverence, mingled with a joyous gratification, that we behold you in our midst to-day. The affectionate reverence needs neither explanation nor comment; the joyous gratification is caused by the fact that we, the members of the Feehan Reading Circle, have long anticipated the pleasure that this hour realizes, the pleasure and honor of addressing Your Grace, and of presenting before you one of our exercises, that you may judge for yourself whether we are keeping the promises made to you, when you granted us the privilege of banding ourselves together under your honored name.

"All the year round Your Grace's portrait smiles down upon us High School boys and girls; from this time, onward to your own Golden Jubilee, may the remembrance of us ever call to your venerable living face a smile of approval.

"It is with varied emotions that we greet Your Grace, on a many-sided occasion, such as this Golden Jubilee day presents, and we rejoice that it is not necessary, amid so much harmony, for us to decide which affords us the greatest happiness, the glory of our parish, the success of our pastor, or the presence of our Archbishop.

The second number was a literary garland of original essays, with the following readers and subjects: "Modern Progress," Frances Fee; "True Advancement," Laura Steffen and Mary Reardon; "Ancient Poetry," Kittie and Clara Killion; "Literature," J. Allen; "Modern Poetry," Helen Burns; "Woman's Pen," Lorine Byrne; "Oratory," John Flanagan; "Shakespeare and Milton," John Scanlan; "Scientific Writers," Louis Knipschild; "Historical Writers," C. Dubs; "Philsophical Writers," John Manion; "Aesthetic Writers," Lizzie Corcoran; "Religious Writers," Clement Gordon and Edward Dubs. These essays were delivered as orations, without paper, and embellished with graceful and appropriate gestures.

The pupils of the school joined in singing a patriotic song, after which Edward Dubs spoke the following Jubilee Greeting to all present:

"As the universe lies pictured before us, by that magic household artist, our imagination, we behold its suns in blazing glory, its planets and satellites in soft radiance, its mighty systems in admirable harmony, all moving majestically in circles; each about its grand centre, each satellite about its primary, each primary about its sun, each sun, with its stupendous system of planets and moons, about some greater sun in distant space, and so on, almost infinitely, circles within circles, until the whole magnificent universe moves, in stately harmony, about the throne of God!

"Circles within circles!—this is the universal plan—this, the unfailing arrangement; this, the prevailing law—that all things shall have a centre about which they shall unceasingly revolve. Had we sharper sight, we could discover, everywhere, an obedience to this law, not only among the vast orbs of space, but among the countless atoms, of which all material things are composed; not only above and around the earth, but on it and in it, would we find this mystic revolution of circles within circles, in obedience to an attraction at the centre. We would behold it in the unfolding of the flowers of spring, in the waving branch of tree and shrub, in the murmuring leaves and in the bending blades of grass, in the rippling stream and in the bounding, crested waves. Motion everywhere, fleet, graceful motion, in obedience to some powerful central attraction.

"Not only in the material world does this beautiful law have force; in the invisible world of thought and sentiment it likewise prevails. The ever-circling thoughts and the ever-revolving emotions of humanity have, too, their powerful attracting centres, exerting an irresistible energy in opposing, with a beneficent centripetal force, the baleful centrifugal force of foreign and dangerous outer attractions.

"Now, in events like those of the past few days, where shall we find the animating principle of all the energy and enthusiasm? What constitutes the centre of all the circling virtue and piety, beneficence and prosperity?

"Turn to what page you will in history, whether sacred or profane, you will find that of every series of events, some one man is the centre, be he king or general, pope or emperor. Now, who is the centre of all that has delighted and impressed you during your sojourn among us? 'The man at the centre' in this case has been, and is, our reverend pastor, the leader of his people, in all enterprising affairs, their model in piety, their guide in all the pathways of civil and religious advancement. Rev. William A. Horan is the 'man at the centre' of all St. Mary's present success and prosperity. Under God, he has been to his people a special providence.

"In making this public announcement of our appreciation of this fact, we, the pupils of the school he has sacrificed so much to establish, desire to honor him and to gratify our illustrious guests, by voicing the sentiments that we feel assured are filling their hearts and minds.

"We most cordially thank our distinguished friends for their presence among us, and we accord them, from our heart of hearts, a thousand loving and reverent greetings."

THE GOLDEN DIADEM; OR, THE JUBILEE CROWN.

(Written expressly for the occasion by a Dominican Sister.)

DRAMATIS PERSONAE.

The Spirit of the Past	Miss Mary Vail
The Spirit of Memory	Miss Annie Summers
The Spirit of Zeal	Miss Alice Cummisford
The Spirit of Holy Vocation	Miss Lizzie Corcoran
The Spirit of Holy Infancy	Miss Kittie Killion
The Spirit of Divine Grace	Miss Clara Killion
The Spirit of Baptism	Miss Laura Steffen
The Spirit of Penance	Master Clement Gordon
The Spirit of the Tabernacle	Master John Manion
The Spirit of Confirmation	Master Joseph Allen
The Spirit of Matrimony	Miss Lorine Byrne
The Spirit of Holy Orders	Miss Helen Burns
The Spirit of Extreme Unction	Master Louis Knipschild
The Guardian Angel	Miss Mary Riordan
The Messenger from the Nations	Master Chas. Dubs
The Messenger from St. Thomas	Master John Flanagan
The Messenger from the Sacred Heart of Jesus	Master John Scanlan
The Messenger from the Sacred Heart of Mary	Miss K. Kavanaugh
The Spirit of Time	Master Edward Dubs

FINALE.

SPIRIT OF THE PAST—DELIVERED BY MISS MARY VAIL, '95.

In hours of meditation, in chance moments of deep reflection, it is upon the Past that the mind dwells; it is from the Past that humanity learns the grave lessons of moral responsibility, and acquires the wisdom wherewith to meet its difficulties, or to support its weight. The consideration of the past brings to human hearts the greater portion of their joys and of their sorrows. It is the past that we celebrate to-day; a past full of sacred significance; a past that gives to our present all its higher meanings; a past that must give to our future its richest values.

Come, then, holy spirits, sister spirits, join me in weaving a memorial crown in St. Mary's honor, on this, St. Mary's Jubilee Day. Since, of precious metals, or of precious stones, we cannot make it, we will give the gems of noble thoughts, in a golden setting of loving and enthusiastic expression.

R. SHERIDAN.

JOHN TRACY.

A. J. McCOY.

JAMES DARRAH.

THOMAS GRANT.

MEMBERS OF COMMITTEES.

I am the Spirit of the Past, ever within call of the beautiful faculty of the soul named Memory, and ever obedient to her behests. Does she wish to warn the heedless, or caution the guileless? She turns to me to picture for them the fate of others, like unto themselves. Does she wish to recall some wanderer, who has wofully strayed to dreary pathways? She demands of me to picture for him the darksome consequences that have befallen others, who have walked in the shadows of sin. Does she long to comfort, strengthen and encourage the despondent soul? She entreats me to depict, with my magic brush, the scenes of a life and a death that were devoted entirely to man's temporal and eternal welfare; a life that was a divine model, a death that was an infinite ransom.

On this occasion, I may surely claim the first place, I and my sweet interpreter, Memory. Our friends are here assembled to celebrate events that we have cherished for half a century, and all the sacred ceremonies of the Church have been presented, with stately solemnity to commemorate them. Come, then, fair spirits, let each one contribute to the universal joy that pervades St. Mary's parish, by the utterance of holy greetings and sacred histories, of joyous behests and happy promises.

What has my guardian spirit, sweet Memory, to say on an occasion that is all our own?

SPIRIT OF MEMORY—DELIVERED BY MISS ANNIE SUMMERS, '95.

As I look backward, through the magic glass of reflection, each beautiful division of the half century, so memorable for St. Mary's people, lies bathed in the golden light of God's special love and benediction, and gleams, with the splendid flashing of brilliant gems, of earnest human endeavor and saintly effort.

Fifty years in the life of a parish constitutes a majestic record for Memory to keep! Only God and His angels might gratify, to the full, the holy inquisitiveness of a devoted people, as to the lives and the deeds, whence came the princely value of those years.

That the half century has glided into eternity, laden with immeasurable merits for many a faithful soul, we may not doubt.

G. W. FARNUM.

C. A. McNAMARA.

T. D. OSBORNE.

J. B. J. DuFOUR.

F. CHAS. DONOHUE.

MEMBERS OF COMMITTEES.

It is my sweet privilege, as the Spirit of Memory, to recall the sacrifices of the early missionaries, the sacred memories of St. Mary's pastors, holy men of valiant lives and noble deeds; the earnest efforts of the Sisters, devoted women, animated with lofty zeal; the generosity and fidelity of St. Mary's good, whole-souled, pious people, men and women, known far and wide for a living faith, supported unflinchingly by a sublime hope and an ineffable charity.

Ah, the visions that Memory pictures, in each mind, to-day, are they not wonderful, in their transitions from log huts, with deal tables for altars, to stately stone temples, with tabernacles of marble and onyx and beaten gold—transitions, from the congregation of ten or twelve individuals to that of two or three hundred families? Ah, yes, this is Memory's own fair feast and joyous festival, and the angels of heaven join with her, in chanting glad hymns of thanksgiving and hosannas of exultation.

THE SPIRIT OF ZEAL—DELIVERED BY MISS ALICE CUMMISFORD, '95.

What were this earthly home of ours did not the blessed sunlight warm it into life and beauty? Where then the verdure? Where then the glowing hues of flower and fruit? Where the thousands of life-supporting products? A wide waste of desolation and horror would lie, where now are spread smiling plains and gleaming waters, where now are grass-grown, snow-capped mountains and sunny, fruitful vales.

What the sun, with its life-giving, life-sustaining warmth and light, is to the world of nature, that Zeal is to the world of earthly spiritual existence. Zeal warms the heart, enlightens the mind, inspires the free will of man and fructifies his soul. Where Zeal radiates its blessed light and heat, there will there be noble growths, of exalted virtue, and a rich abundance of the fruits of true charity.

This band of gracious spirits would be imperfect indeed, without the presence and active assistance of the fervid, the enthusiastic, the dauntless Spirit of Zeal.

Without Zeal, there would not now exist even a priesthood, much less a hierarchy, in this broad, new land. Had Zeal not breathed her spirit into human hearts, there would be no Archbishop of Chicago to-day, to receive our loyal greetings; no Rev. Fathers to represent religion, in our Jubilee Celebration; no missionary priests, and no first Mass to be recalled with joy and veneration; no succession of revered pastors, at St. Mary's, each to be remembered, on this occasion, for having aided, with all his heart, mind and soul, in the gradual advancement of St. Mary's Church, from the small frame building of '45, to the present beautiful structure.

The new St. Mary's, in particular, had its origin in the Zeal, the wondrous Zeal, of a united priest and people. But even Zeal, with all her ardor and her strength, could not have accomplished the grand work that receives it crown to-day, had there not been the closest and holiest union between priest and people, pastor and parishioners.

Let it be my part, then, in the memorial meeting of Jubilee Spirits, to inscribe on the tablets of future fame, with the name, "St. Mary's Church," the significant words, "Zeal" and "Unity."

SPIRIT OF LIFE—SUSIE STEFFEN.

To me, the Spirit of Life, belongs the noble office of attending newly created souls; immortality's beginning, it is mine to bless.

It is an hour of solemn import that marks the beginning of a human life, a mysterious hour when, from nothingness, the soul springs forth, in obedience to the divine voice, and enters a frail human body to abide there, during the brief span of infancy only, or for some longer portion of the promised three score and ten years of earthly existence.

From those dread regions, whence the creative power of the heavenly Father calls the animate and the inanimate, the mortal and the immortal, there came forth the happy, blessed band of noble souls who, as an especially privileged congregation, have wrought the Golden Diadem of St. Mary's honor. Animated by me, and making the best use of the gifts that I offer to all with whom I dwell, they have merited, and have received, certain priceless treasures, reserved for a certain few, who make of life a

holy joy to themselves, and a precious benefit to others. With
delight do I join this band of radiant spirits assembled to honor
St. Mary's Jubilee Day.

GUARDIAN ANGEL—PERSONATED BY MARY RIORDAN.

When you, fair Spirit of Life, having committed to human,
mortal bodies ineffably precious, immortal souls, winged your
way in return to heaven, we, Guardian Angels, left the celestial
abode, and, having taken our flight to earth, stood, in obedience
to God, as a guard about those beings to whom you, great Spirit,
had brought the royal gifts of life and immortality. In memory
of that sweet mission, and of the sacred intimacies of the human
soul with our spiritual being, during the years of nobly spent
lives, I stand among you to-day to aid in forming St. Mary's
Jubilee Crown.

SPIRIT OF BAPTISM—REPRESENTED BY LAURA STEFFEN.

Dear Angel, representative of the guardians of highly favored
souls, I am sure that you forget not that, until Baptism had been
administered to those souls, celestial spirits could but stand beside
them, guarding, indeed, but not embracing. There was a darkness that repelled your brightness; there was a stain that your
spotlessness abhorred; but when the mystic waters of Baptism
washed away all imperfection, making the soul a child of God
and an heir of heaven, how eagerly you and your companions
spread, about these infant possessors of priceless treasure, your
radiant, snowy wings of pure devotion, of unfailing love and
care. Yes, now you could love those souls, as well as guard them.
In memory of that sacred cleansing of the souls of St. Mary's
parishioners, I offer my jewels for the adornment of the Golden
Diadem.

SPIRIT OF HOLY INFANCY—PERSONATED BY KITTIE KILLION.

Holy Angel Guardian, when the spirit of Baptism had
worked the marvellous change in the child's soul, did you not,
ever after, find me in his heart, me, the pure spirit of his childhood, and were you not happy to meet my inspirations in the

early thoughts of his tender mind, my impulses in the artless emotions of his youthful heart?

Ah, with what joy do I contribute to the celebration of this great day, and to the memory of the children of St. Mary's parish who are now grown men and women, earnest, self-sacrificing parishioners. Happy am I to recall the memory of the infants who have been summoned to heaven, ere they lost their baptismal innocence, and joyously do I congratulate those who have lived to become St. Mary's happy, favored school children.

THE SPIRIT OF PENANCE—PERSONATED BY CLEMENT GORDON.

A heavenly companionship is that of the Guardian Angel with the Spirit of Baptism, but alas, it does not continue. With youth there comes the awakening of strange new powers, in both the spiritual and physical being, strange new impulses fill heart and soul. The war of life begins. In passive bliss of innocence and in perfect peace, the infant has been growing stronger, in all those qualities that are to make its youth a warfare, wherein the soul is often wounded. And where or how shall spirit, invisible and intangible, be healed?

Our band of militant souls, and our choir of triumphant spirits, the subject of to-day's joyous greetings, met in their simple forest or prairie homes but few spiritual enemies, and they were but feeble ones. Yet slight as were the wounds, from them received, only one healing was permitted, and that was sought in the Sacrament of Penance. Sweet is the memory of those humble accusations and of those bravely fulfilled penances which purified the souls of the faithful men and women of olden times, when log huts were our temples, and the sacraments were conferred amid the simplest surroundings. Let these memories find an emblematic place in the Jubilee Crown, which, without them, would have only one gem, that of Baptism.

SPIRIT OF THE TABERNACLE—REPRESENTED BY J. MANION.

True, sadly true, gracious Spirit of Penance, is it that in every human life there comes a day when the Angel Guardian, glorious, heavenly spirit though he be, has no longer the power to shield the human soul from danger. Over man's free will, he has only the power of whispered persuasion; he cannot, unaided, still the tempest, nor stop the deadly strife, that youth and its attendant circumstances arouse. In early life, the war of the flesh begins, and only with death will it end.

Though frequently wounded in life's battles, in penance the soul is healed; but something more is needed; to be a victor in strife, to earn the conqueror's crown, the soul must be not only purified but strong. Strong, not only in the power of external aid —be it that of angels even—but with the strength of holy, interior grace, the invincible strength of God-given power. This strength, this grace, comes to the soul in the reception of the Holy Eucharist.

The First Communion means to the faithful soul the beginning of an eternal communion with God in heaven. Among your memorials, then, none will be so magnificent as mine, that of the Spirit of the Holy Eucharist, that which finds a place in the Golden Crown as a sacred memorial of the many souls that have received their First Communion in, both the old and the new St. Mary's Church.

THE SPIRIT OF CONFIRMATION—PERSONATED BY J. ALLEN.

A child of God, an heir of heaven, a communicant in God's choicest gift, the Body and Blood of His divine Son,—it would seem, surely, that even divine generosity could go no further, but it is infinite, and has for the human soul another great gift. Life is a season of strife; the child of God must be likewise a soldier of Christ; the heir to heaven must fight for his birth-right; for these reasons is the Holy Paraclete sent to abide in the soul; for this reason does the Sacrament of Confirmation present to the soul its special graces and blessings. In the Golden Crown, then, do we place remembrances of the visits made to St. Mary's Church by holy bishops, to call down into her parishioners' heart-temples, the Holy Spirit of God, in Confirmation.

THE SPIRIT OF DIVINE GRACE—PERSONATED BY CLARA KILLION.

A wondrous office is mine; to await the divine choice, and then to carry, to the favored soul, God's message; to await the selection made by the Eternal King, from among the children of men, of certain highly favored souls, to be marked for special service on earth and a special throne in heaven.

The divine selection having been made, I, as did the Angel Gabriel, centuries before me, make his glorious visit to the blessed Mother of God, took my flight to earth, and remaining invisible, yet tried, in many a mysterious way, to gain the chosen soul's consent to God's design in its behalf, for even the choice of God will not constrain the soul's free will.

In memory, then, of the ready consent of holy missionaries and faithful priests to my widespread calls and inspirations, I place, in the Jubilee Crown, my sacred memento.

HOLY VOCATION—REPRESENTED BY LIZZIE CORCORAN.

When, after her successful mission to earnest young hearts, the Spirit of Divine Choice returned to the throne of God, and showed there that she had found, in those hearts, naught but loving reverence for the divine will, then was I, the Spirit of Holy Vocations, sent to whisper the divine message, to the favored souls, that my sister spirit had selected, in accordance with the divine command.

In the beauties of nature, in the loveliness of art, in the serious expressions of spiritual books, and in the simplicity of private prayer, as well as in the splendor of public ceremonials, I portrayed, whispered or wrote the divine inspiration, and impressed upon heart and soul, the glowing characters of a most holy, most noble and most happy selection, the vocation to the priesthood.

The response to the call was immediate and generous; the vocation was welcomed, with joyous reverence, was received into the deepest depths of holy, grateful love. A tribute, then, do I pay to the hour of choice, and to the ready response of the faithful priests who have, in the past fifty years, served at God's altar, in St. Mary's Church.

THE SPIRIT OF ORDINATION—PERSONATED BY HELEN BURNS.

Since the moment of man's fall, since the beginning of his immense debt to God, there has been need of a form of religious service presenting, not only adoration, but reparation; expressing not only love, but penitence; offering not only worship, but sacrifice.

This was not attained in the offering of finite victims, on altars of fire, but, in the old law, such worship was the best that man had to offer. After the coming of the Redeemer, this was changed; priceless riches were at man's command, the Body and Blood, Soul and Divinity of the Saviour; thenceforth, man was enabled to offer a sublime sacrifice, the eternal Son of God being the infinite victim, first on Calvary's cross, and, ever after that, on the altar, in the daily Mass.

For the offering of this superlatively acceptable worship, only highly favored and singularly gifted beings might be chosen —chosen to be ordained priests—priests of God and of His holy Church—men to be, thenceforth, stamped, in the soul, with a special character, which neither time, nor eternity, might obliterate.

None know, better than I, the Spirit of Ordination, what are the wondrous changes, interior and exterior, which are wrought in the honored soul by the consecrating hand of the Bishop. All previous graces and blessings were granted, with a view to this mystic hour, the hour of ordination. To this peculiar consecration had the purification by Baptism referred, so that where another was simply freed from the stain of original sin, this soul was further adorned with special graces and blessings, whereby it might, from infancy to manhood, be always fitting itself for its high destiny. In the reception of the Holy Eucharist, for the first time, this soul received its call; the Divine Guest, in the boy's heart, whispered the sacred message, the first inspiration, awakening the first inclination towards the noblest and holiest of vocations.

For the hour of ordination, the Holy Ghost, likewise, in Confirmation, gave special light, grace and strength to the soul, and, for that same hour, the Guardian Angel set about it special safe-guards, to shield it from everything that might impair its fitness for its high destiny.

Fifty years have passed since that glad morning, when the Holy Sacrifice was offered, for the first time, in our county. Fifty stanzas of a noble psalm have since been chanted in the church of God, chanted in tones low and faint, at times, when the burden of life was pressing heavily; faint, but discordant, never! Solemnly, reverently, harmoniously have the fifty stanzas succeeded each other, delighting the ear of God; and loud, clear and musical have been the voices of St. Mary's reverend pastors, as they have joined in this wondrous psalm. Some of them are now chanting the triumphant hymns of heaven; all have been true to the grace of Ordination, loyal to their chosen vocation and faithful in the fulfillment of its sacred duties.

THE GUARDIAN SPIRIT OF THE SACRAMENT OF MATRIMONY—REPRESENTED BY LORINE BYRNE.

Since we are all assembled here, we, the Spirits of the Sacraments, it were not well for the voice of holy Matrimony to be silent. Let it, then, be mine to recall the many occasions, in fifty years, on which the golden bands of a heaven-appointed union were clasped with the Church's most solemn benedictions, and most vigorous powers; a union never to be severed, by man below, or angel above. Blessed forever be the marriages that have taken place in St. Mary's sanctuary, during the fifty glad years that we celebrate to-day; blessed the families, the excellent parents and happy children, that have formed, and do now form, a part of St. Mary's highly favored parish.

EXTREME UNCTION—PERSONATED BY LOUIS KNIPSCHILD.

Gloriously have you all portrayed the special and sacred beauty of the sacraments of which you are the Guardian Spirits, and I would not wish that a single word were weakened, or that a single expression were less enthusiastic, for wonderful are the Sacraments of God's Church, but the beautiful chain that you have formed would be imperfect without my link—yes, sadly, deplorably imperfect—for without this link the chain may not reach, beautiful and holy as it is, to heaven's portals, for though Extreme Unction is not absolutely necessary to salvation, yet is most efficacious in procuring for the Christian, who receives it, the grace to die well.

How consoling is the thought of the great numbers of devout souls to whom that holy sacrament must have been administered in St. Mary's parish during fifty years—administered by those who have themselves, long since, departed to the happy realms of eternity.

My spoken tribute is paid to the memory of those of St. Mary's parishioners who went to meet their judge with the blessing of Extreme Unction purifying each of their senses; to the memory, likewise, of those faithful priests who, by means of this sacrament, conferred, through the power given them by God, the stupendous grace of forgiveness of sins and of spiritual health.

MESSENGER FROM THE NATIONS—PERSONATED BY CHARLES DUBS.

This grand meeting of Jubilee Spirits would be imperfect without my presence, and your memorial greetings would lack a distinctive feature without my message.

I bear, to each and all, the greetings of the nations, Ireland, France, Germany and America, which have given of their noblest and their best to afford to St. Mary's her bands of saintly priests and her assemblies of devoted people, during the long space of fifty years.

From patriotic, suffering and poetic Ireland; from brilliant, enthusiastic and ever friendly France; from strong, thrifty, philosophical Germany, and from vigorous, free and generous America,—I present greetings, most joyous and most significant, as seen in the light of those past years, when the sons of these countries were St. Mary's pastors, and both sons and daughters were St. Mary's parishioners.

MESSENGER FROM THE SACRED HEART—REPRESENTED BY JOHN SCALNAN.

From the very throne of God, come the inspirations and messages of the Sacred Heart of Jesus, and only the glowing Seraphim may bear them to the Guardian Spirits, who pass between heaven and earth. Be it mine, then, to repeat what a

Seraph has sweetly uttered, in token of the loving regard of the Sacred Heart for St. Mary's people, so many of whom practice, with unfailing fervor, the pious requirements of the Holy League.

May not much of the parish's prosperity, and the congregation's fidelity, be traced to the wonderful promises made by our Lord, through the Blessed "Margaret Mary," to those who shall faithfully follow the practices of devotion to the Sacred Heart? Many are the wise deeds of true friendship which your pastor's love for your immortal souls has prompted him to do for you, but in none has he been wiser than in having established among you a branch of the League of the Sacred Heart, for, thereby, he has afforded you the means to become spiritually strong, and has set about you a fortification against the enemies of your souls.

To-day, we doubt not, there has come, from the glowing depths of that all-loving Heart, special greetings and special blessings to St. Mary's pastor and his people.

MESSENGER FROM ST. THOMAS AQUINAS—PERSONATED BY JOHN FLANAGAN.

St. Thomas Aquinas, "Angel of the Schools," and special patron of St. Mary's children, sends greeting, glad greetings, to all assembled here. With tender watchfulness, he has seen the approach of this memorable day; with special and heavenly delight does he behold its celebration, replete with the logic of events, full of the philosophy of history's best elements. Honored am I to be the bearer of his august message, wherein he, the mighty wielder of magic words, expresses his high regard for the noble philosophy upon which the government and teaching of St. Mary's parish and congregation are based.

Some words of peculiar solemnity and holy meaning has he, on this occasion, for our Rev. Pastor's private ear; these it is not for one like me to repeat nor interpret; to our Rev. Father's heart, will the great and holy Doctor whisper them, and sweet tokens will they be, not only of the Saint's fond regard for a favorite client, but of the sacred love of the Saint's Divine Master for His faithful and truly devoted priest.

MESSENGER FROM THE SACRED HEART OF MARY—
REPRESENTED BY KATE KAVANAUGH.

"Unseen, yet seen," choirs of angelic spirits have hovered, in and about St. Mary's Church, during these glad days of consecration and celebration; unseen by men, yet seen by God, they have done the will of their Immaculate Queen, and have joined their celestial tones with the harmonics of terrestrial voices, in those solemn psalms and hymns, whereby human hearts seek to express their deeper and holier emotions of love and adoration.

Patroness of our church, powerful Protectress of our congregation and our parish—Mary, "Blessed among all people," sends greetings that are echoes of those from her divine Son, and second only to them, in their joy-producing power, and in the sacred effects of their united benedictions.

THE SPIRIT OF TIME—REPRESENTED BY EDWARD DUBS.

The greetings have been all presented; the spiritual history, as it were, of St. Mary's parish has been given; joys and sorrows have been recorded; graces and blessings have been symbolized, and now Time sounds the hour for parting. Each beautiful Spirit will leave gifts of priceless value to be cherished, in the human hearts that have been gladdened by this occasion, or have, which is more blessed, aided to make the hearts of others glad.

May the Spirit of the Past never be called upon to record, regarding St. Mary's people, anything that might tarnish the brightness of Memory's pictures, or dampen the ardor of Zeal's earnest endeavors.

May the Spirit of Life have no cause to regret having brought immortal souls to St. Mary's homes and home-keepers. May there be, in the midst of St. Mary's parish, as many Guardian Angels as there are human souls, and may the Spirit of Holy Infancy dwell with all the little ones of the flock. May the Spirits of Divine Grace and of Holy Vocation be ever busy among St. Mary's people, both young and old. May the Spirits of the Seven Sacraments be as active as, even the Sacred Hearts of Jesus and Mary can desire. May St. Thomas find every member of the congregation obedient to his teachings in all things. May the

Nations be proud of St. Mary's record, and may Time close, for her people, in a blessed eternity.

Let us join in a hymn of thanksgiving, and then take our flight, for which I offer you "the wings of Time."

(The Te Deum.)

THE JUBILEE POEM.

At the close of the above drama, Miss Mary Vail, a post graduate of St. Mary's, read very prettily, the Golden Jubilee Poem, which had been composed for the occasion, in imitation of Sidney Lanier, and ran as follows:

> A rainbow span of fifty years,
> Painted upon a cloud of tears,
> In blue for hope and red for fears,
> Finds end in a golden hour to-day.
> Ah, to us in our childhood the legend was told,
> "At the end of the rainbow lies treasure of Gold,"
> And now, in our thrilling hearts, we hold—
> The gold that will never pass away.
>
> Gold crushed from the quartz of many a crystal life,
> Gold hammered, with blows of many a human strife,
> Gold burnt, in the love of Christian man and wife,
> Till it is pure as the very flame ;
> Gold spun from the love of daughter and son,
> Gold with which every good gift is won ;
> Gold that the patient and the brave
> Amass, in realms beyond the grave ;
> Amass, neglecting praise and blame.
>
> O golden hour is this, that crowns the time,
> Since, heart to heart, like rhyme to rhyme,
> Good people knelt to hear the chime—
> Of holy mass, by spirits rung,
> That tinkled many a sacred secret sweet,
> Concerning how God and holy souls should meet ;
> And whispered of the Saviour's lingering feet
> With a most sacred, silver tongue.
>
> O golden day, of that first sacrifice ; O golden crown,
> For kingly heads and royal hearts, then bowed down ;
> To you no smile, to you no frown,
> Except the smile and frown of heaven ;

Dear heads, some white, some dark with raven hair;
Dear hearts, some gay, some weighted down with care,
What thoughts, what feelings had you there?

Old settlers of this favored place,
To-day you miss full many an honored face,
That would have smiled, with joyous grace,
At this, our Golden Jubilee feast.
But God is good, and God is great,
His will be done, if soon or late,
Our dead stand happy, in the golden gate,
And call our jubilee blessings not the least.
So, friends most dear, and friends most wise,
Look to your jubilee rainbow in the skies,
Grasp the full meaning of the many-hued prize.
Then, with souls as full of joy, as souls may be, we gladly say,
"Holy hearts that wrought with smiles through tears,
This rainbow span of fifty years,
Behold how true, how bright God's love appears."
His holy grace, His priceless gifts, His tender care,
True gold, bright gold, gold most rare,
To make you rich, to make you glad, without alloy,
On this, your Golden Jubilee day, of highest joy.

A pleasant feature of the occasion was the presentation to Rev. Father Horan of $400 in gold, a sum donated by several ladies and gentlemen of the parish. Rev. Father Du Four made the presentation speech, which was feelingly responded to by the pastor, who was the recipient also of a goodly number of other gifts from home and abroad.

A LITERARY CHAPLET.

Woven in honor of His Grace of Chicago, by the Feehan Reading Circle, of St. Mary's High School, on the occasion of the Golden Jubilee.

THE SUBJECTS AND THEIR REPRESENTATIVES.

"True Advancement" .... Laura Steffen
"General Literature" .... Joseph Allen
"Poetry of the Past" .... Kittie Killion
"Minstrelsy" .... Clara Killion
"The Lyric Muse" .... Helen Burns

ROBERT CASEY.

THOS. CARROLL.

MICHAEL SCANLAN.

PATRICK GRANT.

RICHARD HUGHES.

MEMBERS OF COMMITTEES.

"The Epic and the Drama"..................................John Scanlan
"Names Known to Fame"............................Kate Kavanaugh
"Historical Writers"......................................Charles Dubs
"Scientific Writers"....................................Louis Knipschild
"The Power of Oratory"..............................John Flanagan
"American Writers".....................................Mary Reardon
"Woman's Pen"..Lorine Byrne
"Aesthetic Writers"....................................Lizzie Corcoran
"Philosophic Writers"..................................John Manion
"Religious Writers"....................................Clement Gordon
"The Literature of the Church"...........................Edward Dubs
"Modern Progress".......................................Frances Fee

MODERN PROGRESS:—Well, well, I wonder when we will have done with these old-fashioned entertainments, these dull "Open Meetings," these silly so-called "Literary Programs"! I wonder when, instead of this awkward, feminine costume and this poor little stage, we will have a manly garb and rostrums.

A poor way this for displaying feminine ability! Here we are, like so many demure, "Puritan Maidens," prepared to make the prosiest of speeches and the dullest of impressions,—yet, in these electric days, there is need of woman's electric tongue to inspire the public and to direct the councils of the nation; need of woman's magnetic influence to govern the national impulses, to guide the national will, and to direct the national strength.

Here we are at the nation's footstool, when we should be gracing the nation's throne. Study, study, study!—and what comes of it all? What use is it to know that Julius Cæsar and Scipio Africanus, and others like them, were not only great leaders, but learned men—since, however learned we may become, we shall never be leaders?

TRUE ADVANCEMENT:—How absorbing, how blinding is the desire for power! What matters it that we cannot lead? Were it not better that our aim should be knowledge? That the glorious desire "to know" should animate heart and mind?

True Christian advancement consists, in applying our knowledge to the acquisition of those things which benefit man physically, morally and mentally. What are the needs of this lofty being we call man? His magnificent intellect,—it must be developed;

JOHN E. HOGAN.

E. J. SCANLAN.

M. O'BRIEN.

JAS. P. YOUNGER.

J. RIORDAN.

MEMBERS OF COMMITTEES.

his stupendous powers,—they must be governed; his admirable abilities,—they must be made to benefit himself and all his race.

"Progress"? "Advancement"? Thought carries us to the very throne of the Omnipotent, in the hollow of whose hand man lies, infinitely small and utterly insignificant. Yet, so high is man placed, in the scale of creatures, he is ever tempted to advance, rather than to mount.

Dazzled by the magnitude of his own works, he would become a worshiper of himself, only that nature, yielding her secrets with reluctant hand, makes him feel that she is conquered, not by his will, but by his exertions, and that there is a limit to his power, infinitely short of what it might be, did he but aim upward, as well as onward.

Realize, then, O human soul! that true Christian Advancement is not merely the dream of a visionary. Scan the earth; consider the various legitimate employments of its human inhabitants,—is there one of them that precludes the idea of an upward movement, as well as an onward?

Piety does not deaden activity; nature's noblemen are not idlers; they labor, but they do not confine their thoughts to the subject of loss or gain. They are found in all stations of life, and their distinguishing characteristic is loftiness of purpose.

MODERN PROGRESS:—Wonder if she means all that lecture for me? Quite eloquent and interesting, but by no means convincing. "Christian Advancement," indeed—an old fogyism of the middle ages! Haven't I "a glorious desire for knowledge"? Don't I read the newspapers and all the periodicals?

As for "nature's noblemen"—why, they'd starve in our day. What political party would be so mad as to propose one of "nature's noblemen" as a candidate for any office?

Oh, we have no manner of use for them, in practical life. They do very well in poetry, and we build monuments to their honor,—good, solid monuments, that will keep them, and their lofty ideas, from rising up against the true interest of the world!

LITERATURE:—Ours is said to be an age of thoughtfulness. Thinkers are rife in all departments of knowledge, and, so prolific are the writers, the deadly work, of all swords ever wielded in battle, could be buried six feet deep, beneath the work of the pen.

"Who is it that, divested of his robes of flesh, with vision clear and pure, scans the firmament, from star to star, catching inspirations from each gleaming orb? Who is it that, in mental flight, passes from mossy dell to mountain height; from sunlit cloud to running stream; from smiling vales to ocean depths—gathering

J. P. COFFEY.   JERRY GORDON.   M. FLANAGAN.

MEMBERS OF COMMITTEES.

beauties, everywhere, and imprisoning them in a mesh of tuneful words?"

"It is a mighty mind, with swift, yet solemn sweep of magic wings, with intellect of purest fire, accompanied, as is better far, for us and earth, by a human heart, a heart that feels, that weeps and trembles, that speaks our language and responds to our emotions." It is the poet. It is he who grasps a noble pen for a noble purpose.

Literature has not been the least delightful of our studies during the past two years; rather has it been the most interesting and profitable. Let us, then, honor this occasion, and the presence of His Grace, our beloved Archbishop, by weaving a garland in memory of all successful wielders of the magic pen.

MODERN PROGRESS:—Oh, yes; let's talk about literature! Modern Progress has freed Literature from the bondage of former centuries, when Superstition was the counsellor of the nations, and Literature, in return, has become the inspirer of Modern Progress. Why, our very strikers, the leaders of our mobs and riots, have written letters which will be inscribed, henceforth, on the tablets of fame. Oh, yes, Modern Progress approves of Literature; she works for progress; she scatters newspapers far and wide, and makes the world think as Modern Progress thinks.

SPIRIT OF LITERATURE:—Silence, saucy intruder! We must fain notice you at last, and beg you to discriminate between the vile productions of a free-press and those grand eminations of the human mind which the educated and refined call literature.

Dear companions, you who have assembled here, to honor true literature, let us weave our beautiful, symbolic chaplet, in honor of the great minds of the literary world, with flowers culled in their own fragrant thought-gardens, and bedewed with gems, from the deep mines of their profound reflections.

The first offering should be made, in honor of the poetry of the glorious past.

POETRY OF THE PAST:—God said, "Let there be light, and there was light." Thus opened the grand epic of creation. "It is consummated;" thus closed the tragedy of the Redemption, and, from the entoning of the first, to the final note of the last, how many solemn psalms were chanted; how many mystic songs and holy canticles were sung! The poetry of the remote past breathes in the words of Scripture, and bears, as all true poetry should, a message to mankind.

Turning from these sacred themes, and passing, as out of out our sphere, the poetry of Asia, of Greece, and of ancient Rome, we find, in Western Europe, the earliest poet was the minstrel, Troubadour, Trouvere, or bard. Minstrelsy had its birth, not in Italy, land of song; not in Spain, home of chivalry; not in Germany, abode of music; but amid the ruggedness of Scandanavia, the green hills of Erin, and the highlands of Caledonia.

In France, the Trouveres of Normandy, and the Troubadours of Languedoc, sang of daring deeds and of the heroes who did them.

"While the Skalds of Scandanavia celebrated their dwarfs and giants, dragons and monsters, the Troubadours, filled with the genius of Gothic fiction, constructed many a tale for nothern wonder, from fragments of Homer. Imagination pictures an Anglo-Norman court, or baronial hall, with its minstrel holding his listeners entranced as he sings his metrical romances. How natural our sympathy and bond of alliance with the men and customs of feudal times. They were our chivalric forefathers, and, with all their stern, warlike qualities, they wove much of poetry in with their struggles for liberty and justice."

All honor, say I, to the minstrels of old, far above any modern writer of song or play, sonnet or hymn. [Begins the chaplet by placing flowers on the little table in the middle of the stage.]

A TRIBUTE TO THE BARDS: Yes, and every heart melted as the bard recited the woe of stricken knight or forsaken captive, widowed mother or fatherless daughter.

What modern poet has been the inspirer of his people? Who would now dare to sing of past glory, present woe, or future redress, with the hope of being heard in the councils of a nation? He would be expelled from the senate chambers of modern nations, as a madman.

But, in those olden days, the bards were the most honored of the nation's sons. The bards excited armies to bravery and preceded them in battle, when the cause was just. The bards were the heralds of princes, the mediators of peace, the welcome guests of lords and kings.

The voice falters, choked with tears, as we endeavor to portray the pathetic memories associated with the bards of ancient Ireland. Would that Turlough O'Carolan, last of his race, might appear before us, to tell us what it meant to be an Irish minstrel,— to have his part, in the home-life and the heart-life, of all whose thresholds he crossed.

Sweet and sad are the tales, he would tell us, of the tears which he had caused to flow, tears refresing to human hearts. How many the aching heads he soothed, as did all his class, with the sweet music of the harp and the rich tones of his fine voice.

Many, too, were the hearts that beat, high and warm, at his recital of deeds of reckless heroism or of gentle benefaction.

Joyously were the bards everywhere greeted, sheltered and fed; their presence a blessing; their songs a delight; their person sacred from harm, at the hand of even the deadliest foe.

Proudly, enthusiastically, do I make an offering to your memory, O sweet poets of the past. [Places flowers in the chaplet.]

The Music of the Lyre:—Gazing, with my companions, down the aisles of Time's grand memorial hall, listening to her, as she apostrophizes the last of the Irish bards, I seem to see, in the distance, a wonderful procession, headed by one whose brow, like the faces of the knights he has pictured, glitters with the light of noble thoughts.

"So mannerly is he and full of gentle grace,
 Of him every tongue is compelled to say,
 Here's the noblest of a noble race."

Father of the sons and daughters of the lyre, with Spencer, I greet thee—

"Great Chaucer, well of English undefiled,
 On Fame's eternal bead-roll worthy to be filed."

And now my eye is gladdened by a view of him of pure character, elegant culture and genius rare, the "Fairy Queene" at his side and about him the knights of holy names. He stands, as it were, in the light of some rare stained window, glowing with the beauty and the wealth of his own descriptions and imagery.

Following this brilliant group, comes one bowed with grief, but, on the luminous face, sit enthroned genius and resignation, proclaiming him to be Robert Southwell, the martyr-poet.

O wonderful, O beautiful procession of lyric poets! Note them, as they pass along this mystic pathway of recollection,— Young, his mantle gemmed with the stars and the radiance of of "Night Thoughts" on his brow; Thompson, with the flower-garlands and snow-wreaths of "The Seasons" about him; Collins, with the "Passions" writhing beneath his gifted pen; Dryden, with his matchless flow of language, is hastening to "The Feast of Alexander," while St. Cecilia hovers near. There is Goldsmith, "object of our laughter and our love, of our pity and our admiration"; there is Gray, mournful, stately and wise, and Burns, singing his songs of perennial freshness, in the sweetest of dialects; his songs:

> "Which gushed from his heart,
> As showers, from the clouds of summer,
> Or as tears from the eyelids start."

Slowly wending his melancholy way, comes Cowper, dear bard of the hearthstone, his morbid sensitiveness shrinking from the very fame that is, to the poet's heart, so dear.

We know them all so well, these dear spirits; their names household words; their sentiments part of our mental being; it seems scarcely possible that it is almost a century since the last named closed his melancholy career and found in death a peace and rest unknown to him in life.

Once more let us look upon the thrilling pageant—behold! noble, magnificent, scoffing, sneering Lord Byron, the clouds about him, one while darkened by misanthropy, again, illumined by the lurid lightnings of base sentiments and violent passions; yet there is sweetest music, as he passes, so charmingly do the words flow from his magic pen.

Byron gives place to Shelly, another "archangel with his heavenly light obscured"; he is the embodiment of the spirit of poesy, an ungrateful man, using the great gifts of a generous Creator against himself. Then comes Moore, magic song-singer, whose notes thrill every heart, in every land, where the English language is known; Keats, of promise fair and death too early; Wordsworth,

> "To whom the meanest flower that blooms can give
> Thoughts that do often lie too deep for tears";

Tennyson, so great, in his poetic gifts, that even a queen's attempt to honor him did but cast a shadow upon his illustrious name, for *Alfred* Tennyson will ever be almost infinitely greater than *Lord* Tennyson.

We are to make offerings in memory of these imperishable names? Ah, lilies and pearls would I place on Chaucer's breast; glowing roses and flame-like rubies would I cast at Spencer's feet! and thus, as the wondrous procession passes, would I throw, in the pathway of each inspired one, the flowers and gems most like his thought and mode of expression.

THE EPIC AND THE DRAMA:—In your love for the lyre, methinks you have failed to see some of the grandest figures in the wonderful procession of poets. The world is indeed happier, nobler and more heaven-like for the magic gift of song, but could we spare the majesty of the Epic, or the grandeur of the Dramatic poetry? Lo, in the procession you have described, as Spencer's brilliant group, and Southwell's heavenly face pass away, there appears—a king! ruler in a world sublimely intellectual, yet a world where exists the affections, the passions, the moralities and the anxieties of real life. A king? We might more aptly call him a creator, who waves the magic wand of his literary skill, and calls into existence beings of every grade of human intelligence and social standing; beings actuated by every degree of human feeling, from the wildest paroxysms of passion, to the softest delicacy of emotion. Volumes would not contain all that may be said of his genius and its wonderful achievements.

We need not name him; all recognize the supreme poet and dramatist, Shakespeare; and who is this that follows Shakespeare so closely? Who is it that, with bowed head, sightless eyes, and a face like one of his own archangels, comes surrounded by visions so magnificent that we may well believe that when overwork closed the eyes of his body to the beautiful things of earth, God opened the eyes of his soul to the sublime realities of heaven.

O Milton! Homer and Dante combined (with much that is all thine own), to thee, and to the matchless dramatist of all time, I pay my tribute of admiration, praise and love. [Places flowers in the chaplet.]

OTHER GLORIOUS NAMES.—The young lady who spoke so eloquently on "The Music of the Lyre," omitted many illustrious names, noted for their owners' skill in lyric verse. As the blind bard is hidden from our view, by his angels and archangels; as they surround him, in passing down the aisles of Time, he disappears, and other forms of dignity and grace present themselves to the imagination.

There is Pope, the brilliant, witty, satirist; Addison, the pure and exquisite, with poor Dick Steele, who is always somewhere near him; Johnson, mighty wielder of stentorian words; Scott, dear, noble Scott, great in poetry, great in prose, and great in misfortune; Coleridge, deep thinker and most instructive and entertaining talker; DeQuincey, unfortunate "opium eater," of wonderful genius and learning; Lamb, with the peculiar charm and subtle beauty of his style; Macaulay, with his magnificently rounded periods, and a host of others. Scatter flowers and gems if you will, but let some of the choicest of your offerings fall at the feet of these giants of the intellectual world.

HISTORICAL WRITERS:—The poets and dramatists do indeed fulfill a beautiful mission, but how dull the world, how useless the faculty of memory, were the voice of the historian silenced.

Behold that man—one moment erect, strong, confident in the years stretching peacefully before him; the next, bleeding, helpless, doomed to silence and the grave. Great in life, surpassingly great in death, how long would this hero be remembered, did not history inscribe his name on the tablets of fame?

"Visit some field after battle, look upon the dead and the dying; they are thrust from this world's interests, from its hopes, its aspirations and its victories, into the visible presence of death. What blight and ruin meet the anguishing eyes of these dying men; what brilliant, broken plans; what lofty, baffled ambitions; what sundering of manhood's strong, warm friendships; what bitter rending of sweet, household ties,— yet they go forth, from this world that is so dear to them, sacrifice these affections that fill them with happiness, and die on the battlefield."

"Should not the hearts of their countrymen thrill with instant, profound and universal sympathy, esteem and honor? Masterful in their triumph over human feeling, should they not become the centre of a nation's love, be enshrined in the prayers of a world?"

It is the historian who records these deeds, and keeps the memory of them beautiful, undimmed and sacred. I pay my tribute, with all the enthusiasm of my heart, to the world's historians. [Place flowers.]

MODERN PROGRESS:—La me! how he does go on. One would think it the most delightful thing in the world to be bleeding and dying, with your limbs lying scattered about promiscuously on the battlefield!

Modern Progress is going to stop all that nonsense; if the nations will not submit to arbitration, why, in our next war, we shall have electrified automatons do our fighting, while we contemplate the bloodless field, from an air-ship.

SCIENTIFIC WRITERS:—Your impertinent interruption reminds me of a class of authors that we have, thus far, overlooked. Is it just to forget the writers on science? Writers whose pens have been as keys, unlocking for us the gateways to discovery and invention? With what sublime simplicity they dwell on the grand phenomena of natural philosophy and astronomy, on mathematics, Godlike science of numbers almost infinite, on geology, thrilling history of our planet's growth.

I lay my tribute at the feet of the scientists; mighty discoverers of nature's secrets and wonderful powers; masters are they of the magnificent forces that are daily making and remaking the world.

MODERN PROGRESS:—Scientists? Why, yes; they are my best friends, and the deadly enemies of my old enemy, Superstition. Yes; I approve of Science and its writers.

SPIRIT OF SCIENCE:—What do we care for your approval? The science of which you approve is not the hand-maid of Religion, mother and queen of all true Sciences.

The masters, to whom we have referred, esteem it their noblest privilege, and highest honor, to sit at the feet of Religion, and to be taught by her.

THE POWER OF ORATORY:—It is claimed that the pen is

the mightiest instrument in the world, and, indeed, its power is great, but no writer has exerted the same irresistible influence as the great speaker.

"What can surpass the power of an orator? How he captivates the understanding; impels or restrains the will of whole assemblies."

"Give a man earnestness of purpose, and an eloquent tongue, the inclinations of the people bend before him, as the grass before the wind. Give him enthusiasm and eloquence, he will inflame the heart, fire the will, illuminate the understanding of each listener in a multitude, and at the bidding of this one man, many men will die, for the cause which his magic tongue has told them is just."

A tribute of honor to the English-speaking orators, in every land, and in every age, it is my happiness to present, and in memory thereof, I place this emblem in the Jubilee Crown. [Places flowers.]

MODERN PROGRESS:—Truly is this an age of much speaking, and speech-making is much pleasanter than the performance of uselessly grand deeds.

AMERICAN AUTHORS:—You poor, restless Spirit, you seem yourself to be possessed of the modern tendency to windy speech-making.

Sister-Spirits and Brother-Spirits, is our own dear land of freedom too young to have its men great in the realm of letters?

Does not Literature, as well as all things else that are good and fair, gain glorious existence under "the stars and stripes"?

Shall we, when paying our tributes of honor, forget Franklin, Jefferson and Hamilton, the glory of our colonial age, or fail to see Audubon, surrounded by the American birds he loved so well to describe? Can we pass, unnoticed, such names as Adams, Madison, Channing and Allston?

Is there, in English Literature, a fairer memory than that of the boy of eighteen whose mind was of so serious and profound a character as to produce "Thanatopsis"? Tenderly and reverently let us follow Bryant, through all his spotless career, him who was the "Father of American Poetry," the poetry of nature, at once our Chaucer and our Wordsworth.

In imagination, we look upon him; his face, uplifted, bears the expression of one whose thoughts are always dwelling on pure and lofty themes; his glance is one of reverent observation, ever fixed on nature's beauty and charm; his heart, so his lovely old face, as well as his poetry, tells us, is full of deep religious feeling, a feeling that ever dictates pure and lofty expression to the classic dignity of his pen.

Turning, reluctantly, from Bryant, we gaze with fond affection upon our other silver-haired minstrel, dear Longfellow; his name a household word, his poetry an ever increasing delight, particularly sacred to the Catholic heart, which finds, on Longfellow's pages, so many beautiful poems of which the Church was the inspiration.

Not far away, we see Whittier, so fierce in his denunciation of wrong, so gentle in his tenderness for the right, so strong in his charity and love.

Sunny-tempered, laughter-loving Dr. Holmes—how much joy he has caused to exist, in hearts and homes, honored forever be his memory! And there is Lowell, the many-sided, the many-gifted, the unsurpassed; Poe, the brilliant and erratic; Saxe, the oddest of humorists; Read, poet and artist; Boker, poet and banker; Lanier, sweet southern song-bird, and Father Ryan, above and beyond them all, in many respects, though all are worthy singers to the music of the lyre. Many a sweet-voiced songstress, too, might be mentioned, did time and space permit.

In the field of prose, who have scattered nobler seeds than Irving, Prescott, Bancroft, Cooper, Hawthorne, Emerson, and, that giant among them all, O. A. Brownson?

To the memory of America's writers, then, I offer a wreath of her own fair flowers, their fragrance is not purer, sweeter, richer than the sentiments and expressions I intend them to symbolize and to honor. [Places a wreath of wild flowers around the base of the crown.]

Modern Progress:—Well, of all the nonsense I ever listened to! Not a word about our truly great men, our millionaires; nor about their daughters, who have done so much honor to America, by marrying into the English nobility.

Poets, indeed! Useless men, in a busy, progressive country, such as this. Luckily they have died off pretty fast of late years.

Woman's Pen:—Could the sick, the weary or the afflicted spare the touch of woman's hand, or consent that the gentle tones of her voice be silenced? The hand that ministers to the weak and the suffering, yet manages household affairs, need not be less skillful in wielding the pen. Noble and blessed, in every sphere, woman has not failed to fulfill highest duties in the world of letters.

"Since the days, when the mother of Samuel proclaimed God to be the Lord of knowledge and the Giver of understanding, since the days when Miriam, the sister of Moses, taught sacred canticles to the young Israelites in the temple, there has been no age without women among its scholars, its warriors and its writers of song." Nowhere do we find the beautiful realized, with more vividness, simplicity and grandeur, than on the pages of the female writers of various periods of time, and of many lands.

"A woman's impulses are naturally heavenward in tendency, hence the gift of poetry is for her a great, a noble instrument, used for a sublime end." Would that I had an offering of the purest and most fragrant lilies to lay at the feet of the female writers of every literary epoch. [Put flowers in the crown.]

Modern Progress:—Who are these old-fashioned women you are quoting to us? To be sure, the warriors are all right; woman should be able to fight her own battles, but, between times, I'd have her at something better than writing poetry. Not poetry, but politics, should be the field for her wonderful abilities.

Aesthetic Writers:—Do not turn from me in disgust, because my subject suggests sunflowers and all things a-la-modern culture, or because the term culture is so often misapplied to weak artificiality.

"There has been much eloquence expended on 'diamonds in the rough,' but we know that it is the refined and cultured who give most pleasure to others, and themselves find in life the highest delight. It is the cultured taste that rejoices in all things high and pure; that gathers, from all sources, the rarest treasures, wherewith to enrich the mind wherein it dwells. The aesthetic writer is quick to conceive ideas of loveliness and perfection, that another could not grasp.

"The most profound learning, the most varied acquirements, could not compensate for the absence of culture and refinement. To the cultured ear, all sweet sounds of nature are music, and music itself a rapture. To the cultured eye, all things in nature are fraught with meanings ineffably sweet and infinitely sublime. To the truly cultured heart, no just appeal from nature, art or humanity, is made in vain; such a heart ever responds with magical sympathy and an elevating influence." Refinement, like disposition, is natural; true Christian culture, like virtue, must be acquired; yea, acquired, as are habits of virture, by making "stepping-stones of our dead selves to higher things." To the truly refined and cultured I pay my tribute. [Places flowers.]

MODERN PROGRESS:—Making "stepping-stones of one's self" must be miserably disagreeable! If to be gloriously uncomfortable is to be cultured, what a lofty mind and refined heart Diogenes must have had, when passing his delightful days under a tub! I wonder—is he the patron philosopher of aesthetic writers and cultured readers?

SPIRIT OF CULTURE:—Begone, rude Spirit! Falsely calling herself "Modern Progress," she has held a place among us too long. Come, True Advancement, give me your assistance, and we will banish her from our court and company, where she has shown herself merely a noisy intruder. [Culture and Advancement lead her from the stage and then they return to their places.]

PHILOSOPHICAL WRITERS:—The tribute to heroes on literary fields would be imperfect, were we to forget the writers on philosophy—that grand, subtle, mysterious science of the mind and its wonderful faculties.

Philosophy is the discoverer of all scientific laws, the creator of all inventions, the interpreter of all historical events, and the solution of all the problems of nature. Without it, language would be a mere confusion of words, and literature a snare.

"In philosophy, all theories find either a proof or a refutation, for it analyzes all sensations and corrects all perceptions. It controls, moderates and guides the most enchanting pleasure of life, the use of our reason. It dictates to us how we shall, with fidelity of memory and brilliancy of imagination, impart light and knowledge to other minds. All science is the field of its conquests; all art the application of its principles."

"The illumination of an age does not consist in the amount of its knowledge, but in the broad and noble principles that govern and actuate the people." Now, of all universal laws, of all broad principles, and of all grand ideas, Philosophy is the inspirer, and has her place, next to Revelation, in the Temple of Faith.

From the lofty mountain top of thought, the Christian Philosopher views the entire stream of harmonious truths, and rejoices in the revelation they are of the infinite mind of God; rejoices that there is a progress and an advancement, an upward and an onward, which include a clearer knowledge of God and a nearer approach to His infinite perfections.

To Christian Philosophers I pay my tribute of honor, admiration and praise. [Places flowers in the chaplet.]

RELIGIOUS WRITERS:—During all the beautiful school year, we have learned no lesson of which God was not the Alpha and Omega. No page of history, no stanza of poetry, did our eyes rest upon that we did not read, between the lines, the story of God's love and the hymn of His glory.

It is fitting, then, that we commemorate the glorious work of Religious Writers; fitting that we recall the productions of those noble minds that ever aim at a close union with the eternal mind of God. They have dictated, to glowing pens, words of highest, holiest meaning, messages of ineffable beauty and lessons of priceless worth. From the days of the stylus and waxen tablets to these pens and printing presses, there has been no age not glorified by the writings of the scholars and saints of the Church of God.

To these I make my floral offering of reverent affection and highest esteem. [Places long-stemmed flowers in a vase standing in the middle of the garland.]

DEFENDERS OF THE FAITH:—In every department of literature we find them, these noble "defenders of the faith"; these high-minded philosophers, dignified historians, brilliant essayists and sweet-voiced lyrists—all, either announcing, defending or adorning the Truth. All filling the mind with high thoughts, the heart with generous ambitions, the soul with noble aspirations.

I do not name them, these great ones, the minds capable of appreciating them know them; the hearts they have instructed and strengthened love them; the souls they have inspired with a holy enthusiasm bless them.

Priests and religions, their debtors, for some of life's sweetest, richest and most sanctifying hours, hold them in reverent regard, as true friends and monitors, while we, too young yet to fully appreciate them, hope to know them better in the bright future.

We now place, above all your offerings, ours to the Religious Writers and to the Defenders of the Faith. [Places long-stemmed flowers in the vase standing surrounded by the chaplets, which rests, finished, on the table.]

SPIRIT OF LITERATURE:—We have done well, sweet Spirits; we have banished false Progress, and we have completed our fragrant, bright-hued chaplet, emblematic of the unfading beauties and imperishable perfumes of spiritual and intellectual delights.

Ere we part, let us join in a glad hymn of thanksgiving. [They sing and then depart.]

"The Jubilee Spirits" is orginal, and was written by one of the Dominican Sisters, expressly for the occasion.

"The Literary Chaplet" is made up of essays, partly original and partly adapted from various sources; it, also, was arranged by one of the Sisters teaching in the school.

The manner in which the pupils of St. Mary's High School acquitted themselves, in presenting these difficult essays, was highly commendable, and elicited praise from every one in the vast audience, before which they appeared with so much ease and grace.

Few features of the Jubilee Celebration afforded Father Horan so high a degree of pleasure as this tribute from the children of his beloved school, for, though it was not possible to bring the various classes together, in vacation, to practice anything dramatic, they all joined in the singing, so that each pupil of each department contributed to the enjoyment of the occasion, and was thereby personally gratified and honored, having, too, the pleasure of storing away the event, in the memory, for future delectation.

At intervals, between the vocal and the oratorical contributions, Masters Charles, Clement and Peter Gordon, also Miss Mamie Gordon, gave choice instrumental selections on piano and violin.

How the Great Event was Celebrated at St. Joseph's Church.

At St. Joseph's the jubilee services were of a very impressive character. The Rev. Father Kalvelage celebrated solemn high mass at 10 o'clock, as Bishop Messmer did not arrive. He was assisted by Deacon Rempe, as deacon, and the Rev. Father Meyer, as sub-deacon. Father Meyer delivered a sermon that was very appropriate, and truly eloquent.

At 3 o'clock in the afternoon, Archbishop Feehan administered the rite of confirmation to a class of about one hundred and twenty-five, ninety from St. Joseph's and the others from parishes in the vicinity.

On Sunday, at solemn mass, the choir sang Wigard's Mass, in honor of St. Joseph, and were assisted by the St. Pius' Orchestra. Sopranos, Mrs. J. H. Siefelder, Mrs. C. Drexlar, Misses Josie Metz, Tillie Redlinger, Nellie Trunck, Clara Straub, Cornelia Steffen, Ida and Sophie Secker, Alma Kautenberger, Clara Secker and Anna Tappe; altos, Mrs. Theresa Tappe, Mrs. Julia Cavanaugh and Miss Nellie Steffen; tenors, Messrs. Stephen Bucher, A. E. Wiencke, T. Kinzig and P. Kautenberger; bassos, Ernst and John Tappe and Fred Rodemeyer. Orchestra, R. Luecke, 1st violin; Ed. Rotzler, 2nd violin; P. Vodecka, clarionet, J. A. Siefelder, double bass; Gustav Ullrich, cello.

The introit, gradual, offertory and communion were Gregorian, and in keeping with the Feast of the Exaltation of the Holy Cross.

The services in the evening were followed by an eloquent sermon, by the Rev. Father C. Danz, of Mayence, Germany, which was listened to by a congregation that filled the church to the very doors. Benediction of the Blessed Sacrament closed the sacred celebration.

The decorating of St. Joseph's Church for the Golden Jubilee services was very beautifully and artistically done. Between the windows, on the side walls, depended festoons of white and yellow bunting and ropes of evergreen twisted together, while long strips of drapery and ropes of evergreen were caught up to the high ceiling. The choir-loft rail was similarly dressed. The richest decorations were within the chancel rail; above the sanctuary lamp swung a large anchor of white and gold, while the altars were almost hidden with flowers, every niche having its vase, and on each projection was hung a wreath. Both inside and outside of the rails, were banked foliage plants and pots of flowers.

Among Father Kalvelage's guests were Bishop Messmer and Bishop Janssen, also several priests. The first service, on Sunday, was at 7 o'clock, and at 8, the Right Reverend Bishop Messmer celebrated Low Mass and administered Holy Communion. At 10 o'clock, solemn High Mass was celebrated, and in the afternoon Archbishop Feehan confirmed a large class of boys and girls.

Monday morning, the Jubilee services began with a Pontifical High Mass by Bishop Janssen, and a sermon by Bishop Messmer. In the evening, the parishioners joined in the parade, after which there was a sermon at St. Joseph's Church, by the Rev. C. Danz, of Mayence, Germany. In conclusion, Benediction of the Most Blessed Sacrament was given.

Religious and Literary Associations attached to St. Mary's Church.

The benefits arising from the association of persons with similar ideas have always been recognized by the Church; her sodalities, and her religious communities, existing as they have in every age, are sufficient and illustrious proof of this wise adaptation of worthy means to still worthier ends.

In every well organized parish, then, are to be found societies of various kinds, carrying out the good purposes of zealous pastors and earnest parishioners. St. Mary's, an example in all else, is not wanting in this particular; she has her excellent youths and virtuous maidens, her faithful men and pious women, banded together, in a number of associations, admirable alike for their large membership and their zealous undertakings.

The Holy Name Society, established by the Dominican Fathers, during a mission given by them, in 1890, boasts a membership of about seven hundred men.

The Married Ladies' Sodality, or Altar Society, has ninety members. The officers in this, the Jubilee Year, are: President, Mrs. K. Stanley; vice president, Mrs. P. J. Lonergan; secretary, Mrs. L. Thro; treasurer, Mrs. J. Rau.

For purposes of lawful amusement, and to counteract the evil influences of worldly associations, the Columbus Club was formed, soon after Father Horan became pastor of St. Mary's. To it belong the gentlemen of the parish between the ages of sixteen and seventy. They have a well equipped hall, where they may enjoy manly recreations, without fear of injury to themselves or their neighbors; here they may assemble, for amusement, at any hour they choose, but they have a regular society meeting once a month.

The Young Ladies' Society of the Blessed Virgin numbers fifty active members, out of a hundred registered, and, in union with the Married Ladies' Sodality, constitutes the "Altar-Fund Association," which is responsible for the debt on the main altar. This altar would have been donated, by the heads of two families, but the pastor desired that all the parishioners should have the benefit of the Mass to be offered twice a month, forever, for those, in the parish, or elsewhere, who make a monthly donation of twenty-five cents, for three years, towards the payment of this debt.

These two sodalities, sometimes singly, sometimes in union, have accomplished many valuable services for the parish. Both are ever prompt, zealous and successful, in responding to any call made upon them, or their funds, by the pastor, in behalf of the church, or in the cause of charity.

St. Thomas' Sodality, to which all the school children belong, has been referred to, at length, in the chapter on St. Mary's School, but we will here add that no sodality has been more zealous, nor has any accomplished more good deeds, for God, and for souls, than this band of pure, loving young hearts.

St. Mary's Dramatic Society, with its talented young members, has distinguished itself by a series of dramatic and musical entertainments of a high character, both as to the nature of the programmes presented and the skill of the performers of the several parts. The officers, under whose efficient direction this association has won such an enviable name, are as follows: President, Rev. L. X. DuFour; vice president, Mr. Jas. O'Rourke; secretary, Miss B. Knipschild; treasurer, Mr. Ed. Lawless; stage manager, Mr. J. L. Carroll; press agent, Mr. J. Rau; properties, Mr. A. Lagron.

At the time of the Golden Jubilee Celebration, St. Mary's Choir surpassed its always honorable record, and so distinguished itself as to elicit praise, from even the severest musical critics, hence its members were so encouraged as to undertake even higher and better work than in the past.

With a view, then, to musical improvement, and to the acquirement, not only of increased skill, but of a general knowledge of music and its beautiful history, the members of the Jubilee Choir have formed a duly organized association, under the title of "St. Cecilia's Choral Union." The officers are: President, Rev. W. A. Horan; vice president, A. Lagron; secretary, Maggie Carey; finance secretary, Jennie Tracy; treasurer, Mary Brennan; librarian, Mrs. M. Ellsworth; directors, Frank Rogers, Ed. Lawless, Annie Summers, Mrs. L. Thro, Jennie Tracy.

With a membership of forty ladies and gentlemen, gifted with a love for music, and powers for contributing to its production, the union promises much for the improvement of its members, and the enjoyment of those whom it will, from time to time, be pleased to entertain.

In addition to the varied character of the associations already named, there are several of a purely spiritual nature, which have a flourishing existence in St. Mary's parish. These are the League of the Sacred Heart, whose faithful members make each first Friday of the month a holyday, as it were, and the Arch-confraternity of the Most Holy Rosary, whose members rejoice, on the evening of each first Sunday of the month, in witnessing the beautiful Rosary procession, as it winds its sacred way, through the aisles of the church, to the sound of sacred hymns.

Thus does St. Mary's Church become indeed, a veritable vestibule of heaven, where men and angels mingle, in sacred, loving familiarity, praising God on high and helping man on earth; helping man to elevate his mind and heart above the level, whereon he is forced, for a time, to dwell.

Nothing is more conducive to the frequent reception of the sacraments, and to the formation of habits of piety, than these religious associations. They are the mainstay of a congregation, the foundation of its present stability, and the assurance of its future permanence.

The Closing of the Jubilee Celebration.

The festival of the local Catholic Churches, commemorating the fiftieth anniversary of the establishment of the faith in this county, was brought to a close on the morning of Tuesday, Sept. 16, with a solemn requiem mass, for the souls of those who, in the early days, banded together in the first congregation. For it was they who made generous contributions, from their slender means, and sacrificed their time, and their labor, for the sake of their faith, thus originating two large and flourishing parishes. Splendid edifices have succeeded the simple chapel in Mrs. Egan's humble home, and the rough and unpretentious little church which was built later; but the faithful members of these new congregations do not forget the toil, the efforts and the self-denial of those who have gone before them, and have already heard the blessed words, "Well done, good and faithful servants!" Those early pioneers were not forgotten in any of the festal celebrations; their memories were revered, and praises of their hardihood and loyalty were sung, again and again. In coming to untrodden lands and making for themselves homes, in the forests and on the prairies, in developing the new land, for their own comfort, even, they did far more, for the generations who were to come after them, than they did for themselves, and it was a fitting tribute to them that the last solemn services of a festival, made possible, by their well directed efforts, should be one for their peace and rest.

The weather had done its worst the day before, still the parade and the meetings, which were the closing events of the day, were great successes; had it been at its best, it is difficult to estimate how many more would have taken part in the demonstration. The parade, under all the difficulties that the weather afforded, the unpleasant streets and the damp atmosphere, was one of which the two parishes may feel justly proud. There were one thousand or, one thousand two hundred men in the line, which stretched its length over nearly a mile. All along the route were gathered crowds to witness the procession, and on Stephenson street, the sidewalks were blocked by thousands who cheered the passing lines. The rain kept at home many delegations from parishes in the vicinity, who would have otherwise attended, but still there was a fair number of outsiders in the parade.

The procession was formed at the arch, in front of St. Mary's Church, at 7:30 o'clock; those from St. Mary's parish who took part fell in, modestly, behind the St. Joseph's societies, as the latter marched past the arch. The formation and line of march was as follows:

Marshals and Assistants.
Henney Buggy Company Band.
St. Aloysius' Society of St. Joseph's Church.
St. Pius' Society.
St. Joseph's Society.
St. George's Branch C. K. of I.
Members of St. Joseph's Congregation.
Madison Band.
Columbus Club of St. Mary's Parish.
Holy Name Society.
Members of St. Mary's Congregation.
Visiting Delegations.
Shannon Band.
Mayor and City Officers and Speakers in Carriages.
Clergymen and Visitors in Carriages.

From St. Pius' Hall, on South Galena Avenue and north on State Street to St. Mary's Church, where the procession formed at the arch and went north to Williams, west on Williams to Chicago, north on Chicago to Galena, west on Galena to Cherry, north on Cherry to Stephenson, east on Stephenson to Adams, south on Adams to Galena, west on Galena to South Galena Avenue, south to St. Joseph's Church, whence St. Mary's delegation proceeded to their headquarters.

The two head marshals led the way and the Henney Band followed. In the line were three floats; on these Greek fire was kept burning. The first represented the log house, where mass was first said in Stephenson County; the second displayed a wheel, with fifty golden spokes, about which were grouped fifty small boys, and the third showed a painting of the present St. Mary's Church. There were also two other floats, from which fireworks were shot continually. All those in line carried lanterns swung over their shoulders. The different societies carried their banners, and a handsome national flag was borne in the front rank. Following the line of men on foot, were carriages, in which rode the mayor, the city officers, the visiting church dignitaries, and the clergymen resident in Freeport.

The officers in charge were: J. J. Sweeney and Frank Rogers, marshals for St. Mary's; Fred Rodemeyer, head marshal; M. Zimmerman, standard bearer; C. M. Mueller, marshal, and Joseph Redlinger, standard bearer for St. Aloysius' Society; Robert Schwarz, marshal, and John Steffen, standard bearer for St. Pius' Society and the Catholic Knights; John Weimer, marshal, and John Murdaugh, standard bearer for St. Joseph's Society of St. Joseph's Church.

When St. Mary's delegation reached headquarters, there was a short concert by the Madison Band and more fireworks were burned. One of the large floats was placed in the middle of the street, and used for a platform from which the address of the evening was delivered. There was an immense crowd, fully 5000 people, present; these packed the street for a block either way. Rev. Father Horan presided, and on the platform were the Rt. Rev. Bishop Burke, a number of priests, and Hon. M. Stoskopf, besides the orator of the evening, the Hon. James F. O'Donnell, of Bloomington.

Before introducing the speaker, Father Horan thanked the members of St. Mary's and St. Joseph's Churches, the Catholics of the county, the clergymen who had come to take part in the ceremonies, and the citizens of Freeport generally, for their aid in making the jubilee festival a success.

When Mr. O'Donnell was called on, a modest looking young man stepped forward, and after saluting the Rev. Fathers, at once began his address without preface. His first sentence brought a round of applause, that was repeated every time a slight pause in his rapid delivery would permit it. As a speaker, Mr. O'Donnell is fluent and eloquent, and his flow of words was unbroken by a single hesitation. His rhetoric is graceful and polished, and each point in his address was made forcibly. As he proceeded with it, his face became animated, and his voice, clear and distinct, enunciating every word perfectly, reached to the farthest limits of the immense audience. He gesticulates freely and with dramatic force. The address impressed every one who heard it as one of the finest oratorical efforts they had ever listened to, and, at the close, the young speaker was warmly congratulated, by bishops, priests and laymen.

After his salutation to those on the platform, he said:

"I am expected to say something on Catholic citizenship. To be a good citizen it is not necessary to be a Catholic, but to be a good Catholic it is necessary to be a good citizen; so let me rather take the broader view, and speak on American citizenship.

"The simple law handed down by Justinian, time cannot improve: 'Live honorably, hurt nobody, render to every one his due.' In the affairs of life, the hammer of ambition falls upon coveted gold and silver, shaping them into useful forms and beautiful. In the affairs of discourse, the silver of speech and the gold of silence fall upon the tongue, marring or beautifying companionship, according to the discretion we employ. Society can have harmony and happiness only through a proper deference for knowledge. We all should read more; our views would expand; we would become more considerate of the opinions and feelings of others; we would become nobler and better men and women. In our reading we should not be restricted by prejudice; we should read all sides, not with a feeling of hatred for that which does not conform to our views, but we should be ready to accept truth whenever it presents itself. Let me add, that if those who feel not well disposed towards the Catholic Church were to read more of her history, they would find in it an elevating and beauti-

HON. JAMES F. O'DONNELL.
The Lay Orator.

ful lesson, worthy of something loftier than to be the target for misinformed assailants. I know all in this beautiful city—all in this magnificent audience—are broad and liberal. If others were present, I would say: The less a man is informed on Christianity, the less he appreciates that boon, good-fellowship; the less the milk of human kindness courses through his veins, the more he abominates a Catholic. So, Catholicism, beautiful as is thy name, grand as are thy precepts, would that I could summon before me thy vivifying virtues, and not repeat thy name, for I would speak to defend and not offend.

"I am decidedly unworthy of even talking on sacred subjects, but I realize that there are those who regard us as slaves of superstition and ignorance, when our faith is an inspiring, an ennobling study, hand in hand with Scripture and wisdom; when it is really their own lack of information that leads our opponents to misjudge us. Sane men will all agree that truth is the one thing sought in all sciences; the one thing which should be sought in all spiritual as well as worldly affairs. Now, it is a philosophical principle that that which changes cannot be true. We get the same beautiful idea in this passage from Julius Cæsar: 'Constant as the northern star, to whose true, fixed and resting quality there is no fellow in the firmament; the skies are painted with unnumbered stars; they are all fire and every one doth shine, yet there is but one in all doth hold its place.' In this we see our Church. So it is with the world; 'tis furnished well with men, and men are flesh and blood and apprehensive, yet in the number I know but one that, unassailable, holds his rank unshaken by motion. In this we mean the head of the Church on earth, with St. Peter as the foundation stone, and to whom Christ said: 'Thou art Peter; upon this rock I will build my Church, and the gates of hell shall not prevail against it.'

"This unchangeableness from the time of Christ, we think, is in beautiful keeping with truth. The wise teachings of St. Peter and his line of followers, history shows, have never been in error; and while we respect the opinions and esteem the talents of all who differ from us, yet this fact remains a pleasant fortification to all who cherish Catholic belief.

"I am sorry to think that, despite the blaze of intelligence shed upon the world by the Catholic Church, in astronomy, mathematics, mechanics, electricity, galvanism, chemistry, optics, thermetics, mineralogy, botany and all sciences; despite her liberal and instructive influences, there is a regretable prejudice held against her by many well meaning people. Think you Cardinal Newman, the brightest and purest mind of his day, whose conversion to the Catholic Church, after years of fervent study, turned all Europe topsy-turvy—think you, he would have accepted that faith, if it were in any way faulty? Think you Cardinal Manning, that intellectual giant, the working-man's guiding star, would have joined the Church if it were in any way offensive? Would America's great literary light, after tasting of the teaching of all creeds—I refer to Brownson, would that towering intellect finally have attached himself to the Holy Roman Catholic Church if it were weak in any of its precepts? Look at the roll of honor she has given to the world: In oratory, who surpasses Chrysostom, Daniel O'Connell, Edmund Burke, Daniel Dougherty or Bourke Cochran, now one of the master orators of the world? Among warriors, we have Joan of Arc, Henry Hotspur, Henry IV. of England, Richard Coeur de Leon, Talleyrand, the firey Napoleon, Pulaski, Lafayette, Sheridan, Shields, Mulligan, Meagher, Norton, John Barry, Rosecrans, DeMontcalm. In literature, we have Dante, Shakespeare, Fenelon, Dryden, Pope, Racine, Francis Assissi, Lingard, and Sir Thomas More. Among the painters we have Michael Angelo, Raphael, Murillo, Giotto, Fra Angelico, Donata, Ghiberti, Gregori. In music we have Mozart, Beethoven, Liszt, Hayden. On the stage we have Modjeska, Sarah Bernhardt, Mary Anderson, Rose Coghlan, James O'Neil, Florence, Salvini. Lawrence Barrett did more to elevate the modern thespian art than any man of his day, and Goethe, though not a Catholic, in his wonderful production of Faust, shows the two extremes, the wine room and the Catholic Church, and shows Mephistopheles recoiling from the sword that has a handle in the shape of a cross.

"If you dislike Catholics, do not look up to the star-studded sky, for it was a Catholic, Copernicus and Galileo, who led the retinue in exploring the firmament and giving names and habitation to the heavenly bodies. Throw away the calendar that counts the time, and from which we get the day and date of the week and month, for it was a Catholic Gregory who created it. Ignore mathematics, for it was a Catholic Francis Viete who gave us algebra as we have it now. If you are unkind to Catholics, turn not to the rainbow to drink in its beauty as it spans the sky, for it was a Catholic Descartes, founder of modern mechanical philosophy, who was the genuine author of the explanation of that dazzling and rapturous arch in the heavens. Look not on the thermometer as you feel the chilled air of night, for it was Catholic Sanctorius who made the first. Dispense with the telegraph, telephone, electric cars and electric light, for it was a Catholic Galvani, Volta, Gramm and Carre who were the fathers of the science of electricity. Lay aside chemistry, for a Catholic, Antoine Lavoisier, was the father of its modern form. Destroy the flowers in the field that scent the air, for it was Catholic Caesalpinus who was the father of modern botany. Stop the pulsations of your heart, for it was Catholic professors who enabled Harvey to discover the marvellous circulation of the blood. Disregard the fossils in the rock-ribbed earth, for it was a Catholic De Vinci who first gave them attention.

"If you are unfriendly to Catholics, forget your tongue, for it was a Catholic Chaucer, who was the author of the language we call the richest in the world. Forget your country, for it was named after a Catholic, Americus Vespucius. Forget Columbus, who discovered your country, and accomplished the greatest and grandest event known to all time, and forget forever that stupendous fair in Chicago, which was in honor of his memory, for Columbus was a Catholic.

"Now, I say all this, not in a spirit of boastfulness, which is always contemptible, but because it is natural that it should be a pleasant recollection to all in whose veins flows Catholic blood. Other creeds have their sublime environments, and all come in for full respect; for opinion, like patriotism, is strong in all of us. Some writer says opinion is more powerful than the fear of bodily pain, or death; as appears in studying duelists, gladiators and soldiers; as appears, also, regarding religious devotees and martyrs. It is more powerful than the desire between the sexes, as appears in the more sacred love between brother and sister. It is more powerful than the love of friends, as appears in the duelist, who, to his opinion, sacrifices the life of his friend and exposes the widows and children to misery. It is more powerful than a mother's love for her child, as appears in India, where a mother throws her child to the sharks in the Ganges, or in this country, where a misguided young woman destroys her infant, the pledge of her misplaced love. Then in religion and politics, should we not be tolerant? Give me that man who has studied the history of his own country and of other countries, and is broad enough to appreciate that the people of no country, and the people of no creed, were free from the mist of ignorance that belonged to past centuries; who believes in the fatherhood of God and the brotherhood of man, and who looks up to that broad, blue dome as the ceiling of our common earthly home."

In continuation, Mr. O'Donnell spoke of the beauties of American citizenship, eulogizing the broad-minded men of all faiths, who had kindled and kept alive American liberty and principles. His address was liberal and patriotic, giving evidence of a well-stored mind. His peroration was a brilliant burst of eloquence. In closing he paraphrased Tom Moore's immortal lines—

"You may break, you may shatter the vase of will,
But the essence of 'liberty' will cling 'round it still."

When he took his seat, the applause lasted for several minutes, until some one suggested, "Three cheers for O'Donnell," and they were heartily given.

There was a call for the Hon. M. Stoskopf to make a speech, and he responded very briefly, complimenting the Catholic people on their celebration, and paying a tribute to Father Horan, the members of the parish as citizens, and Mr. O'Donnell as an orator. The meeting was ended by the Madison Band playing the national anthem.

There was an appropriateness in the selection of the Hon.

James F. O'Donnell, as the layman to deliver the address at St. Mary's Golden Jubilee Celebration, that was not developed until after he had accepted the invitation. The Rev. Father O'Gara, the third priest of St. Mary's Church, and one of the best beloved and most zealous of all, was his great uncle. Mr. O'Donnell was the colleague of the Hon. M. Stoskopf at the last session of the legislature, and the two are warm friends. He is a young man, having been born in Dubuque thirty-two years ago, and for a short time, in early childhood, lived here in Freeport. Some of the older members of the parish recognized him. It is likely that Mr. O'Donnell will speak here again in a short time, and if so, a reception will be tendered by the Columbus Club.

The St. Vincent Orphan Asylum.

So many and so beautiful are the phases of charity in the Church, that we behold her hand outstretched with a mother's love to all forms of misery and distress. Let suffering or sorrow appear, in any guise whatever, she is ready with her tender ministrations, comfort and relief, accomplishing her sacred tasks in the manner that is wisest and best.

It is her holy charity that has dotted our land with hospitals and asylums, thousands of which are now stately buildings, with all the modern appliances for cure and for comfort, but which orginated in the Bethlehem of the divine Master, in simplicity and poverty. Never do the holy ones of the Church, those entrusted with affairs nearest to her heart, wait to make a grand and impressive beginning. The Master began with a stable, for the temple wherein He was worshiped, by the simple, the humble, the illiterate, and He ended with St. Peter's incomparable cathedral at Rome, where all the world may come, and where the greatest and mightiest have knelt, in awe-struck adoration.

St. Vincent's Asylum for Orphans is then in the Bethlehem stage of its existence. At present, it is a frame cottage, pretty, bright and pleasant, but simple, as becomes the infancy of a great undertaking; but the future will, no doubt, see this tiny home of loving devotion to Christ's little ones replaced by towering walls of brick and granite. Be that as it may, the present condition of the asylum and its innocent inmates is most encouraging, and all, who are interested, see in it the promise of a glorious future.

The grounds, adjoining those of the hospital, are, like them, considerably higher than the surrounding country, thus affording pure air and an extensive view of charming scenery. With a frontage of 160 and a depth of 300 feet, the grounds surrounding the asylum will afford ample space for the erection of a larger and more imposing structure, when the time for it arrives, as it undoubtedly will, in the near future.

In the meantime, tiny infants, four of them yet in the cradle, and small children, both boys and girls, are receiving, at the hands of the devoted Sisters, the tender, motherly care of which death had deprived them, until they were so happy as to have found their way into this haven of peace and safety.

The property was purchased in the spring of 1896, and the institution was opened to admit its first beloved inmate on Penticost Monday, of the same year. On May 25th, it was formally and solemnly blessed.

Twelve orphans, boys and girls, under ten years of age, constituted the first family that gathered in this home, afforded them by the faithful members of the Church, and by her self-sacrificing, religious, the Sisters of St. Francis, three of whom are in constant attendance at the asylum.

When the little cottage shall have disappeared, to make room for a more imposing edifice, and the twelve inmates of the cottage shall have multiplied to a hundred, yet will there be no greater peace and joy for the little ones than now, for it is the love that surrounds them, as an atmosphere, that constitutes for them in life all that is worth having; that love which no palace can increase and no abode of poverty decrease.

ST. VINCENT'S ORPHAN ASYLUM.

Parish Customs.

When we study a great people, or trace the development of a nation, our interest centres in the customs of one and the laws of the other, for in them will be mirrored the character of the individuals practicing the one and governing the other. Whatever is true of large bodies of men, is true of smaller communities, hence we deem it well, in giving a history of the parish, to mention the daily, monthly and yearly customs, important factors in the sanctification of the people.

The daily Masses, one at 7 and the other at 7:30 a. m., are never omitted, though the hour for the second one varies, as may suit the convenience of families having funerals or weddings, for both these solemnities, by a law of the parish, must take place during the Holy Sacrifice.

On the greater number of these occasions, a Solemn High Mass (with three priests) is offered, not that the pastor receives so frequently the large honorarium customary in wealthy parishes, in large cities. However poor and simple the departed parishioner may be, if he was remarkable for fidelity to his peculiar duties, as a practical Catholic, and if he sent his children to the parochial school, he has the honor, and the spiritual benefits, of a Solemn High Mass at his funeral, even though his surviving friends may not have a dime to offer towards the extra expenses.

It was a source of constant edification and frequent bewilderment to the editor of this work, when a stranger in St. Mary's parish, to behold such stately funeral services taking place, as a matter of course; as it is an ordinary occurrence, it no longer excites surprise.

On Sundays, in summer, the Masses are at 8 and 10 a. m.; in winter, at 8:30 and 10:30. Except for a few Sundays in August, the last service of the morning is always a High Mass, and the children's choir, its members selected from among the pupils of St. Mary's School, sings at the first Mass. At each Sunday morning service there is a formal sermon, and in the evening, the whole year round, on Sunday, the Rosary is recited and Benediction of the Blessed Sacrament given. For a part of the year, Vespers are chanted, the boys in the sanctuary singing alternate verses of the psalms and hymns with the grand choir. Every Sunday afternoon, there is a meeting of two or more of the religious and benevolent associations existing in the parish. On the first Sunday, the Married Ladies' Sodality meets at 3 p. m., and the Columbus Club at 4. On the third Sunday at 4 p. m., the Young Ladies' Sodality of the Blessed Virgin Mary recites the Office of the Immaculate Conception, after the same form as that used at the Holy Name Cathedral in Chicago. The older members of St. Thomas' Sodality (those who have made their first communion) meet to recite the Office of St. Thomas at 2 p. m., on the second Sunday of the month.

No child not attending St. Mary's School is permitted to belong to St. Thomas' Sodality. The pastor never fails to be present each Sunday at the meeting of whichever Sodality is assembled. He always gives an instruction on these occasions, and then repairs to the club room to assist at a meeting of the Business Men's Committee. This is an important body in the parish, for while acting in perfect harmony with the pastor, and deferring most cordially to his opinion, they are responsible for all the financial affairs of the parish, for which reason their meetings are frequent, important and rather laborious.

Here, as in all well ordered parishes, baptisms occur on Sunday afternoon.

Two Masses are offered each month for the benefactors of

the "Christian School," as the pastor fondly calls it in his public utterances. Two Masses are also offered monthly for the donors to the altar fund. Each Sodality receives Communion in a body on the morning of the Sunday mentioned for its monthly meeting, and on that morning the pastor offers the Holy Sacrifice for the Sodality in question.

On the first Friday of each month, and on the holy days of obligation, there is a Mass at 6 a. m., for the accommodation of the laborers.

On the evening of each first Friday, there is a service consisting of the recitation of the Rosary, the reading of Act of Consecration and of Reparation to the Sacred Heart, and Benediction of the Blessed Sacrament.

The Rosary Procession, which is a beautiful feature of the evening service on the first Sunday of each month, is formed of St. Mary's school children, from the wee tots in the chart class, to the members of the high school; also the altar boys and two priests. The children's choir and the grand choir unite their voices on this occasion.

Among the annual customs, the Christmas novena ranks high. For nine successive evenings, immediately preceding Christmas, the sanctuary is glorified by the exposition of the Blessed Sacrament, amid many lights, and surrounded by a full choir of sanctuary boys, while at the foot of the altar kneels the pastor.

The novena consists of psalms, prophecies, canticles and hymns, chanted alternately, by the sanctuary choir, the latter supported by the rich voice of the assistant pastor, whose solo parts, in the chanting of the prophecies, constitutes no small part of the charm of this exquisite service.

It is a custom to have a small representation of Bethlehem in the Church during the Christmas holidays. Just above the stable or cave gleams a large star of burning gas jets, and within the evergreen bower, that represents the sacred birth-place, are the usual figures grouped, with unusual taste and with an unusual regard for congruity.

During Lent, the customary devotions, common everywhere, are conducted in St. Mary's. The Repository, on Holy Thursday, is much enhanced in its beauty by the presence of a marble altar.

On Christmas and Easter, the grandeur of the choir service is greatly increased by the accompaniment of an orchestra of from six to eight pieces.

Two triduums are celebrated each year; one for the school children's retreat of three days preceding the feast of St. Thomas Aquinas, and another of three days preparation for the feast of the Sacred Heart of Jesus, during which the women of the parish make a sort of retreat, devoting these three days to more frequent prayer, also to meditation and hearing Holy Mass each morning. The triduum ends with the reception of Holy Communion, on the Feast of the Sacred Heart of Jesus.

Every evening in May, the devout people of St. Mary's congregation, and there are large numbers of them, assemble before the altar of our Blessed Lady to recite her rosary, listen to hymns and spiritual readings in her honor, and to join in the Litany of Loretto.

The children's choir, so often mentioned, is in charge of the music teacher at the Convent of St. Mary's; under her direction they chant a variety of beautiful litanies during the May devotions, and also at the October services, which are held every evening, in that lovely autumn month, in honor of our Lady, Queen of the Holy Rosary.

On the evening of the first Sunday in May, after the Rosary procession, a sacred and very beautiful ceremony takes place. It is the Crowning of the May Queen. At the top of a high pyramidal-shaped structure, which is constructed in the sanctuary for the occasion, is placed a statue of our Blessed Lady. White-robed children stand at the foot of this lofty throne; each one addresses our Blessed Mother in poetic language of love and praise, presents a bouquet of flowers and then mounts to one of the steps on the slanting sides of the structure, until all the steps are occupied, as it were by angels, supported in the air by their wings. The last to speak mounts, to the very top of the throne, and crowns the statue with white flowers, while uttering suitable sentiments in the language of verse. Appropriate hymns are chanted at the beginning and at the close of this beautiful ceremony.

On the occasion of the "Crowning of the May Queen," in the Jubilee year, that is, May, 1896, a flash-light photograph was taken of the scene; the resulting picture may be found in the early part of this volume.

At St. Mary's, of course, as at every church in the diocese, the Forty Hours Devotion takes place once in each year, and is carried out with all the solemnity and magnificence possible to willing hearts and hands.

It is the pastor's custom to visit the sick, the infirm and aged on every great feast day, and on the first Friday of each month, administering to them the Holy Eucharist, for their strength and comfort.

On the evening that finds friends and neighbors assembled around the dead, that the living may be comforted by kindness and sympathy, and that the departed souls benefited by the frequent prayers of many, "gathered together in His name,"—on such occasions, the pastor always appears, at some uncertain hour of the evening, and recites aloud, with the assembled friends, the Rosary of our Blessed Lady.

The many good results of such a custom will be evident to the reflecting mind, but were there no other than the identification of the pastor, in the family's hour of darkness and grief, with all that is kind, sympathetic and helpful, it were worth the slight trouble it entails.

Let the reader judge the customs that exist in St. Mary's parish as he may, he cannot but deem it the height of wisdom for the pastor to be, as is expressed in the Jubilee address, presented to Father Horan, "The man at the centre."

There are few of us who have not watched, with eager interest, the result, when some boy with conscious pride in his superior ability to "throw a stone," has sent one spinning gayly through the intervening distance into the very centre of the pond. Instantly, as it, with the impetus gained by flying through the air, touched the surface of the water, there sped forth, from the centre, a gleaming, glittering, quivering circle of sunlit water, then another and a wider; another, still wider, until they became countless in their joyous hurrying for the shore.

Could there be a better figure of the wide influence of "the man at the centre"? Let the circles of moral, political or social influences once start, on their ever-widening way, they will bound

ELIZABETH GRACE PECK.
First girl baptized in the new church.

CHAS. HORAN DONOHUE.
First boy baptized in the new church.

MARY ELLEN GRANT.
First girl baptized in the consecrated church.

the earth before they stop, and many voices will ask, "Who did this? Who is the man at the centre?"

We have said elsewhere, that what is true of large bodies is very likely to be true of smaller ones. There are circles of influence for the town as well as for the nation. And it is a grand thing to be "the man at the centre" of even small areas of influence, for only God can measure their true extent.

It is a magnificent picture that spreads before the mind, as the imagination portrays the thousands of centres in the Church —popes, archbishops, bishops, priests and religions—from whom are circling forth the noble influences of a stable, heaven-inspired, divinely protected faith.

With that picture before your mind's clear vision, dear reader, we leave you. That there are thousands of records such as that of St. Mary's parish, and of the Church in Stephenson County—records even brighter and grander—does not detract anything from the glory of our brief history, for the work it is intended to commemorate and preserve from oblivion is God's work, and naught that God has instituted or accomplished for the salvation of immortal souls, can be either small or insignificant. Much has been done in our time and our place, to Him be the glory.

ALPHABETICAL INDEX.

Altars, Description of	112
Arch, Triumphal	104
Associations, Religious and Literary	186
Burke, Rt. Rev. J	113
Banquet, Jubilee	104
Children's Reception to Jubilee Guests	145
Church, First in Stephenson County	23
First St. Mary's	40
Old St. Joseph's and Old St. Mary's	52
Choir, St. Mary's and St. Joseph's	64, 92
Jubilee	115
Corner Stone	60
Closing of Jubilee Celebration	189
Consecration of St. Mary's Church	99
Committees, Jubilee and Business	56, 106
Dedication of St. Mary's Church	65
of St. Joseph's Church	85
Debts and Donations	58
Early History of Catholicity in Stephenson County	19
of Catholicity in Illinois	13
of Catholicity in Chicago	15
of Catholic Settlers in Stephenson County	23
Factors in the Life of the Church	9
Feehan, Most Rev., His Address	28
First Mass in Freeport	33
in St. Mary's	34
in Stephenson County	25
in Irish Grove	22
Foundation of St. Mary's Parish	33
Father Horan's Life and Labors	83
Du Four's Life	87
Kalvalege's Life	93
Meyer's Life	96

Golden Jubilee Celebration	99
Day	131
Hennessey, Most Rev. J	133
Hospital, St. Francis	96
Hall, St. Mary's	74
Horan, Rev. Wm	83
Jubilee Celebration	99
Kalvalege, Rev. Clement	95
Parish Customs	202
Mass, Jubilee	114
New St. Mary's Church	51
Old St. Mary's Church	34
Oration, Jubilee, by Hon. J. F. O'Donnell	192
Orphan Asylum, St. Vincent's	199
Record of St. Joseph's Church	88
Reception of the School Children	145
Riordan, Rev. D., Sermon	115
Record of Jubilee at St. Joseph's Church	184
Religious and Literary Associations	186
Rt. Rev. Guests of Father Kalvalege	185
St. Mary's School	77
School Journal, Santa Maria	81

ILLUSTRATIONS.

Archbishop Feehan..Frontispiece	
Hennessey..	111
Arch, Triumphal..	101
Barron, Mr. and Mrs. Thomas......................	25
Bishop Burke..	113
Janssen...	121
Messmer...	123
Barron, Mr. and Mrs..	135
Church, St. Mary's in '36 and '55..................	7
St. Mary's in '38 and '96..........................	12
Irish Grove, Old and New...........................	21
Lena and New Dublin...............................	21
St. Joseph's...	91
Convent, St. Mary's..	81
Choir, Jubilee..	115
Soloists and Singers of Parts.....................141, 143	
Committee, Members of.........................149, 151, 165, 167, 169	
Crowning of the May Queen..............................	109
Eight of St. Mary's Rev. Pastors........................	41
Eight Lady Parishioners of the Old Church............	37
Early Parishioners and Their Wives....................	39
Exterior of St. Mary's School and Hall................	75
of St. Francis Hospital.........................	97
of St. Vincent's Orphan Asylum................	201
of St. Joseph's School...........................	93
Egan, Mrs. C...	28
Five Pioneers and Their Wives............................	35
Father Horan..	85
Kalvalege...	89
Du Four..	87
Meyer..	96
F. Kalvalege..	34
D. Riordan..	119

Gen. Geo. Jones, of Dubuque 24
Hogan, Miss Mary... 22
Interior of St. Mary's Rectory................................. 69, 71
        of St. Mary's School................................ 79
        of Joseph's School.................................. 94
        Mary's Church at Jubilee............................ 103
        St. Joseph's Church at Jubilee...................... 105
Mansfield, Mr. G. S... 73
Murphy, Mr. and Mrs. P. H..................................... 77
O'Donnell, Hon. Jas. F.. 193
Pictures of Noted Parishioners................................ 61, 65
Pictures of Well-known Parishioners....................... 45, 47, 50, 53
Rear View of St. Mary's Rectory............................... 67
Side View of St. Mary's Church and Rectory 65
Seven Pioneers.. 27
Staff of "Santa Maria".. 82
Three Famous Infants.. 207
Wall, Mrs. M.. 37

www.ingramcontent.com/pod-product-compliance
Lightning Source LLC
Chambersburg PA
CBHW020829230426
43666CB00007B/1163